the

student kitchen

survival handbook

The essential guide to living away from home

Salma Conway

summersdale

THE STUDENT KITCHEN SURVIVAL HANDBOOK

Summersdale Publishers Ltd
46 West Street
Chichester
West Sussex
PO19 1RP
UK

www.summersdale.com

Printed and bound in Great Britain

ISBN: 1-84024-535-2
ISBN: 978-1-84024-535-6

the
student kitchen
survival handbook

Salma Conway

acknowledgements

eternal gratitude is owed to my mum and dad for putting up with an unemployed layabout 'writer' messing up the house, and for all the expert advice, cups of tea and tireless draft reading. To my sister, Sanam, for the nutrition info and all her wisdom on stinky fridges and toilets. To Richard Porter, for swapping my black pudding for his hash browns, and to Sarah Higgins – a living example of why Hitler should have been a proof-reader. To Kirstin Blomquist and Jessica Sonders for their transatlantic advice, and to the rest of my old housemates; Claire Chapman, Claudia Gilham, Vicky Kent, Carol Finlayson, Hayley Mackay, Ross Pearson and Emily Bevin for all their advice, suggestions and inadvertent inspiration! Finally, thanks to all the students, graduates and elves who contributed with their tales of woe and / or filth.

contents

INTRODUCTION 9

PART ONE

CHAPTER ONE: BEFORE YOU LEAVE HOME.............. 14
Packing for the kitchen.. 16
The Buying Guides 18
Packing is for life, not just for the kitchen 26
Other 'useful' stuff.. 31
And now, a word from our sponsor................................ 35

CHAPTER TWO: A MOVING EXPERIENCE.................. 41
The Devil makes work for idle parents 43
Preliminary reconnaissance 44
The Grocery Buying Guide: basics and variables............. 46
Quoth the raven, 'That's, like, totally mingin', innit. Where's
the chips and that?' 54
Time to say goodbye.. 57

CHAPTER THREE: PRE-EMPTIVE MANOEUVRES........ 59
Storage: A tripartite solution 61
Categories I and II: decisions and consequences 61
Category III: fridge and freezer storage 66
'I'm not a freak, honest!'.. 70

CHAPTER FOUR: AND WE'RE COOKING.................... 72
First things first: create a workspace 73
Bollocks to that, I just want to eat! 76

CHAPTER FIVE: KITCHEN POLITICS............................ 84
Kitchen protocol.. 91
Sud's law 93
Fridge FAQ.. 95

PART TWO

**CHAPTER SIX: LIFE IN HALLS IS LIKE A BOX OF
CHOCOLATES – MOSTLY BROWN AND LIKELY TO
STAIN YOUR T-SHIRT**.. 100
The social scene 102
Networking... 104
Your room... 107
The common room... 112
The bathroom 113

**CHAPTER SEVEN: FROM HALLS OF RESIDENCE TO
HOUSE OF PESTILENCE** 117
Finding a house... 120
The contract and your rights.. 126
Moving in!... 128
Life in the house 131
The kitchen 135
Cleaning the house 138
The bathroom 139
Love thy landlord 140

APPENDIX A: THE SUBSTITUTION GUIDE 144

APPENDIX B: USEFUL RESOURCES 150

Introduction

Congratulations! You got the grades, did the waiting (or the orphan-petting synonymous with the gap year), and soon you'll be off to the heady heights of university life. Or perhaps you are already a university student, which is also very commendable. Either way, you're in good company. The Government hopes that by the year 2010, fifty per cent of all Britain's 'young people' will be receiving a university education. Whether or not that target is met, according to UCAS, the current number of students attending Britain's universities and institutes of higher education stands at around a whopping one million. Throughout the duration of their respective courses, one in four of these students is likely to accumulate a debt of over £11,000, a figure that is set only to rise in the years to come, particularly if the suspected increase in the number of 'chav students' significantly alters the average books-to-Burberry spending ratio.

What does all this mean? The long-term effects of increased student numbers can only be detrimental to the already dire situation that exists in today's student accommodation. In a nutshell, more students means more lazy, inept, downright messy little buggers dirtying up your living space and, most alarmingly, more of the blighters using your crockery and stealing your Jaffa Cakes. Indeed, a nutshell may be all that you have left...

Of course, there is every possibility that you are one of those for whom the prospect of a filthy home, and a filthy kitchen in particular, is not in the slightest bit disconcerting. But the very fact that you are reading this book suggests that you are more likely to be the sort that we shall later identify as the 'kitchen victim' as opposed to the 'kitchen terrorist' (see Chapter Five). Nevertheless, there will inevitably be times when even those with the best of intentions and the cleanest of habits will flagrantly dust their omelette with someone else's black pepper, wantonly pinch a slice of bread or even pilfer a precious tea bag without stopping to consider the inherent hypocrisy of their actions. Desperation mixed with lethargy hits us all from time to time, and this book is here to help you through the pain.

You might be wondering what makes this volume different from the plethora of books already available on 'student cooking' or 'student kitchen diplomacy'. Well, for a start, this is not a cookbook; this is a survival manual. If you are one of those unfortunates who hasn't the slightest idea about how to boil an egg, you will undoubtedly benefit

introduction

from the basic instructions provided by such volumes as Jan Arkless's aptly titled *How to Boil an Egg*. However, if you harbour intentions of cooking anything more complex than a microwavable ready-meal, this book is an absolute necessity. What student cookbooks often fail to address is the fact that you will have to feed yourself three times a day and, more often than not, the mere prospect of having to cook yourself another meal in the conditions available will override even the fiercest pangs of hunger. Cheese on toast again? Oh, no, some bastard nicked all your cheese and yes, the bread is old and mouldy. Before you know it you're reaching for the take-away menus for the fourth time in a week, and, as awesome a prospect as that may sound to some, neither your wallet nor your waistline will thank you for it.

Perhaps you are one of those privileged individuals who will be living in catered accommodation. You might well be under the impression that kitchen protocol is not your concern and, to some degree, you are correct. You will be privy to a delectable smorgasbord of carb-tastic delights every day in the elegant setting of a bustling dining hall. But be warned, the absence of a kitchen and the associated indiscretions therein may result in a shift of negative energy towards living-area and bathroom-based anguish.

Just kidding; you'll have problems in those areas whether you've got a kitchen or not. And let us not forget the joys of moving out of halls and into a student house for your second year, where the condition of not only your kitchen but also your living room and bathroom will be a constant source of sadistic disruption between you and your closest friends (unless your name is Alex Tew and you can afford maids and a butler). It is, therefore, the duty of this guide to offer you some added words of wisdom concerning those aspects of survival, in both halls and house, that exist outside of the kitchen.

So grab a cup of tea (providing you've got teabags, milk and a mould-free mug), make yourself comfortable and take the opportunity to learn from the wizened E. coli dodgers of yore.

part one

chapter one:

before you leave home

So, you're off to university. You're signed up on a degree course taught by delightfully obliging professors whose ambition is to make sure you receive the best and most comprehensive education possible. It may cost you thousands of pounds but, of course, it will inevitably plonk you directly into a successful and lucrative career the second it is finished. And now you're leaving home, your girlfriend / boyfriend has assured you that they love you unconditionally and no amount of distance between you is ever going to change that. You will be together forever...

Now it's six months into the future. The 'transferable skills' you have gained from your university education so far have heightened your appreciation of the subtle nuances of bitterness and sarcasm. The irony of the aforesaid becomes clear.

OK, that was a bit harsh, but the fact is, going to university is a huge, life-altering experience that might be quite different to anything you were expecting. You will undergo phenomenal highs and occasional lows, you will meet fantastic new people that you never imagined existed and you will meet complete bastards who you will wish had never been born. You're about to enter an exciting and alien environment that is utterly out of your control, but the way you choose to deal with what this new life has to throw at you will bring you out of the whole experience as a new and improved person.

What, then, is within your control in all this chaos? Pencils, spoons and teddy bears. Yes, your belongings are your security blanket – they are your lifeboat in a sea of uncertainty. It's important, therefore, to carry out the right amount of planning to ensure that possession and control of your belongings remains unequivocally yours. Never underestimate the effect that losing track of your possessions can have over the rest of your life. If you're busy worrying about who's using your precious frying pan, or why your collection of forks has mysteriously turned into a solo act, when do you get the time to work on becoming involved in debauched little love triangles and accumulating an impressive collection of STIs?

The most simple of things to do, therefore, in order to prepare adequately for the university experience, is to pack carefully: it's as simple as that. So, in the name of all things anally retentive, here is the ultimate guide to packing junk for university. Prepare to be dazzled.

packing for the kitchen

The rules of packing for the kitchen are universal, regardless of whether you're moving into a student village, halls of residence or privately rented accommodation (unless, of course, you're living in catered halls, in which case, you might want to skip this section until next year when you move into a house and you realise how inappropriate was all the whinging you did about the food in the canteen). But before we dive into a comprehensive list of what to take, first we must address some fundamental rules on product guidelines, just in case you go racing to your nearest Swedish Box of Horrors before you've finished the chapter.

cutlery

Knives and forks and spoons. Deadly weapons at 30,000 feet, apparently. In the kitchen, they tend to be elusive little blighters. They go missing, they get stuck in concrete,

Uri Gellar interferes with them. The worst thing is if they all look the same, you might not be sure if your fork is the one poking out of a cinderblock or the one your housemate is using to remove his toe cheese. Bear in mind that you might be sharing your kitchen with up to twenty people. If everyone brings their own cutlery, which they will, then that's a whole lot of cutlery to get jumbled up. But if your knives, forks and spoons have Day-Glo orange handles, then finding them when they are dispersed in other people's bedrooms or other kitchens down the corridor is a cinch. So look for affordable cutlery with plastic or embossed handles – anything that makes them stand out. Alternatively, if you're inheriting your folks' old cutlery, put a little strip of wash-resistant coloured tape at the end of each handle. You won't regret it.

ooh, you look like a right dirty fork

crockery

One simple rule applies to crockery: if you like it, don't buy it. Crockery will inevitably get broken at some point, or if it's lucky it'll get covered in so much mould that it's rendered unwashable and gets thrown away. If you want to keep it safe, keep it relatively small and cheap. Big heavy plates are just unnecessary.

drinking receptacles

Never disregard plastic beakers, but if your lips will touch nothing but glass, avoid the crystal champagne flutes and stick to the absurdly cheap sets of tumblers you can buy at big supermarkets. And when they break, be sure to put all the pointy shards of broken glass straight into the bin so that when it gets emptied, the bin bag splits and your feet get covered in garbage juice. (Yes, people really do this.)

Always bear in mind that the key to shopping for university is finding objects that are cheap but reliable and versatile. For instance, why buy a separate can opener, corkscrew and bottle opener if you can buy a Swiss army knife? Why buy a lemon squeezer when you can squish the juice out with a fork? Why buy any of these things when you can steal them from your parents?

the buying guides

Now we are familiar with a few of the rules, let's take a closer look at precisely what you'll need for the kitchen. The key is learning to balance ingenuity with practicality, so to demonstrate this point, here are two sample kitchenware inventories. They might be called buying guides, but don't forget how many of these things can be sponged off parents and other willing relatives. Study the two, weigh up the pros and cons, then choose your favourite and copy that one.

buying guide I:
'I'm a resourceful son of a gun and I don't care who knows it.'

for cooking and eating:

1 X KNIFE	For spreading, scraping, stabbing, jabbing and cutting up your din-dins.
1 X FORK	For mashing, whisking, pricking, piercing, draining vegetables, squishing juice out of lemons and, erm, eating your din-dins.
1 X DESSERTSPOON	For eating runny things, stirring tea, digging tunnels and eye-gouging.
1 X LARGE PLATE	It's a chopping board, it's a dinner plate, it's a Frisbee, it's anything you want it to be.
1 X BOWL	Cereal, soup, stew, spew…

1 X MUG	For tea, for water, for beer, for life.
1 X SMALL SAUCEPAN	Must have metal handle. For poaching, frying, baking, roasting, boiling, steaming, grilling and drumming with a stick. If it's all metal, it's all good.
1 X SWISS ARMY KNIFE	Sharp knife, can opener, bottle opener, corkscrew... you get the picture.

for cleaning:

1 x SPONGE	With a built-in scouring pad, of course.
1 x OLD T-SHIRT	It's a tea towel, it's an oven glove, it's your mum's and she doesn't know you have it.

the pros

Where others just see a fork, you see a multi-functioning object with the potential to mash, prick, whisk, scoop and drain. You've become streamlined like a castrated dolphin. You've ditched anything weighing you down, no matter how much convenience it may have brought you, and opted for a life of scrupulous ingenuity with minimum baggage. Whilst others dread the terrifying prospect of washing mounds of dishes, you merely have to 'wash the dish' and then you're free to party for the rest of the day.

the cons

People hide when they see you approaching because they just know you're going to say, 'Any chance I could borrow your frying pan?' They all lament the loss of the housemate you defenestrated in a fit of rage for borrowing your fork and not returning it; but on the plus side, they have all learnt not to touch your stuff and they generally stay away from you. You cook alone and you cook for one, you eat alone in a darkened room and most days you just eat SuperNoodles out of your saucepan because your only plate is broken, your bowl is holding mouldy beans in the fridge, and you can't face cooking anything else because it takes so bloody long. Then, in a moment of desperation, one evening you borrow someone else's plate without asking. You use it for your tuna noodle smush, you return it quickly and the theft goes unnoticed. It feels good, so you begin to steal more frequently. With more equipment at your disposal, you begin to try recipes other than pasta mayonnaise. Then, one day, you prepare your gourmet vegetable casserole using a random knife and chopping board you found in the kitchen because the smell coming from the rotting bits of food trapped in your army knife made you heave when you went near it. What you didn't realise was that the chopping board was covered in raw chicken juice and, because you lost your only sponge three weeks ago, you didn't clean it and now you're projectile at both ends. Your housemates throw a party to celebrate.

buying guide II:
'I might not have a swiss army knife, but I don't have salmonella either.'

for cooking and eating:

1 x CUTLERY SET	Including KNIVES, FORKS, DESSERTSPOONS and TEASPOONS. They usually come in sets of six.
2 x LARGE PLATES	You could bring just one of each item of crockery but you'll appreciate the spares when items break or when you're feeling lazy.
1 x SIEVE	More versatile than a colander.
2 x SMALL PLATES	
2 x BOWLS	

2 x MUGS
2 x GLASSES / PLASTIC BEAKERS
1 x MEDIUM-SIZED SHARP KNIFE
1 x PAIR OF SCISSORS
1 x LIGHTWEIGHT PLASTIC CHOPPING BOARD
1 x MEDIUM-SIZED NON-STICK SAUCEPAN
1 x MEDIUM-SIZED NON-STICK FRYING PAN
1 x RECTANGULAR OVENPROOF DISH
1 x MEDIUM-SIZED NON-STICK ROASTING TIN
1 x MEASURING JUG
1 x WOODEN SPOON
1 x WOODEN SPATULA
1 x CHEESE GRATER
1 x VEGETABLE PEELER
1 x CAN OPENER
1 x CORKSCREW
1 x BOTTLE OPENER
3 x SMALL PLASTIC AIRTIGHT CONTAINERS

for cleaning:

1 x PAIR OF RUBBER GLOVES
4 x CHEAP SPONGES (with scouring pads)
3 x CHEAP TEA TOWELS
1 x PACK OF J-CLOTHS

the pros

With this selection, you can cook pretty much anything for yourself without the unnecessary burden of purchasing items

23

that are easily substituted (e.g. using a fork as a whisk or a sieve as a colander). You can cook a variety of food that will keep your diet balanced and your body and mind healthy. You might not have enough equipment to cook for a huge group, but when cooking with friends everyone usually contributes something and smiles and laughter abound. Everyone loves you, and after seeing your economical but incredibly skilled use of kitchen equipment and after tasting your delicious food, they all want to have sex with you.

the cons

You have to keep on top of your washing-up; it's all too easy to get lazy and use every single one of your plates and bowls to avoid washing them. Your good supply of utensils will also make you a target for theft, but after reading Chapter Three, you will be fully aware of how to avoid such peril. So life isn't so bad really. Good for you.

And thus we have established the basics of kitchenware equilibrium. If you're still thinking, 'But what am I going to do without my precious fish knives, casserole dishes and novelty shaped biscuit cutters?', have a read through some of the tips in Chapter Four, or take a look at The Substitution Guide in Appendix A.

a short note about woks

The issues surrounding a wok in the student kitchen are complex. Woks are good. They are versatile and they make a nice stir-fry. But whoever said you can't make a stir-fry of sorts in a frying pan or a saucepan? They get hot easily, they still hold oil – they're just shaped differently. But equally, the wok can be used to do pretty much anything a frying pan or a saucepan can – fry eggs, make curry, etc. The argument seems pretty balanced, until you remember that woks are bloody great monstrosities that take up the entire space in the sink (or on the worktop, where they sit for days full of greasy sminge because they're too frigging cumbersome to clean in your teeny weeny sink). But, you know, it's your decision.

toasters and all things electric

They're all very practical, but if you can't afford to buy them, there will be alternatives. For instance: no toaster? Use the grill. No toasted sandwich maker? The grill or the frying pan will do, although it won't make those cute little triangle-shaped sarnies. No microwave? Use the oven, you lazy sod. No cappuccino maker? Well, now you're just being a ponce. The point is that you don't need to worry about bringing those things with you. Once you get to know your housemates, you can all decide if you want to buy a communal kettle / toaster to keep in the kitchen all the time. If there are enough of you it should only cost a few pounds each, and there's no need to worry about who'll keep it at the end of the year because it'll inevitably be broken by then.

You might even be lucky enough to arrive and find that this stuff is all in your kitchen already. But be wary of a 'water boiling unit' that's mounted to the wall. If you can open it up to look inside you'll understand why; all manner of hideous things can accumulate in there and it's best to leave well alone, unless you want a touch of legionnaire's disease to get you out of an essay deadline.

On the plus side, if you avoid buying the mundane electrical items like toasters and kettles, you can treat yourself to something a little more exciting, like a handheld blender. You can keep it in your room when you're not using it, and it's great for making a whole range of things like soup, sauces, dips, smoothies and cocktails. Plus everyone will love you. Except the person who lives in the room next to the kitchen and gets woken up by the sound of a blender at 4 a.m. when you decide to make a vodka and vodka smoothie.

packing is for life, not just for the kitchen

Now we are familiar with the do's and don'ts of preparing for the kitchen, it's time to think about what else to pack, because – and this may sound crazy – there is life outside the kitchen. The key to packing general living stuff is knowing how much is feasible given the circumstances. If you're moving into a privately rented flat or house then packing can be a little easier, but in halls of residence your bedroom is the only place where your belongings are really secure, and the terms of your let might dictate that you get kicked out every holiday to make way for the more commercially viable conference guests, which means a whole load of packing and unpacking at frequent intervals. So before you leave, you need to get the low down on your situation and pack accordingly. Do your research – phone the accommodation office if necessary and ask them what facilities are available. Does your room have a reading lamp? Is there an iron in the laundry room? Is a duvet provided on the bed or do you need to bring your own? These are things you need to know.

With that in mind, here's a list of stuff you need categorically, with the omission of things like pens and pencils and clothes and a toothbrush because, in all honesty, if you're not aware that you need to pack these things then, well, perhaps university isn't the best place for you right now.

PASSPORT PHOTOS	For some reason everyone wants a picture of you in freshers' week. Four should set you up nicely.
PAPERWORK	Keep all paperwork you have relating to university or your finances in a folder. You will need certain items for registration and, in the unlikely event of your first loan instalment failing to find its way to your bank account, you'll need the relevant documents to hand. Also, write down the numbers you need to call to cancel lost debit cards / credit cards and keep them all in a safe place.
2 SETS OF BEDSHEETS	There is no way on earth you are going to wash your one set of sheets, get them dry and get them back on the bed all in the same day. It just doesn't happen. At least if you have two sets of sheets, they'll get changed at least once per term.
FLIP-FLOPS	You'll understand when you see the showers.
WASHBAG	Again, for the shower.

before you leave home

DRESSING GOWN	For when the fire alarm goes off at 3 a.m.
MARKER PEN	For marking out your territory (i.e. these are my beans, not yours).
ALARM CLOCK	Because early lectures are never easy. Not that this makes them any easier.
STORAGE BOXES	Great for making huge quantities of punch for parties. And for storing things.
COAT-HANGERS	There might not be any in the wardrobe.
FURNITURE POLISH WIPES	Disposable wipes that come in a pack with the furniture polish already on them. So easy there really is no excuse for the inch of dust on your desk.
PHOTOS / POSTERS	Anything you can stick on the walls is good for making you feel at home.
BLU TACK	Obviously.

PAINKILLERS	You'll need them eventually.
TORCH	For when there's a power cut. You'd be amazed at how many people are completely unprepared.
MINIATURE SEWING KIT	Because Mummy isn't there to replace your buttons any more.
CONDOMS	The Student's Union will usually thrust bucket-loads of free condoms in your face throughout freshers' week. These are fine, but if you want super reliable free condoms, they hand them out like candy at the family planning clinic.
PIGGY BANK	Keeping pennies isn't a waste of time any more – most big supermarkets have a change counting machine these days, turning your mass of pennies into legitimate beer money. You pour all the change in and you get a receipt to be redeemed at the counter. They take a small percentage but it goes to charity.

DIARY / FILOFAX	For organising your rock-and-roll lifestyle. Yeah.
USB MEMORY STICK	These things are a godsend. You can keep your essays in one place but edit them on any computer. And it's small enough to stick on your key ring!
BACKPACK / HOLDALL	Not just an essential for packing, but also handy for taking clothes to the laundry room, and even for trips on foot to the supermarket.
INSURANCE	It's essential to get the contents of your room insured, since student residences tend to be a target for opportunistic thieves. There's a whole load of companies that offer very cheap contents insurance to students. Do a search on the Internet, or visit your bank and enquire about their services.

other 'useful' stuff

Now all the necessities are out of the way, it's time to think about those other little essentials that you just couldn't live without. Or could you? From the good to the bad to the just plain unnecessary, choosing what to take from the following list can seriously affect your social life.

extension cord

Most rooms only come with one or two wall outlets, so if you're planning to take anything more than a reading lamp you'll undoubtedly need an extension cord with multiple plug sockets.

camera

What would the university experience be without a million photos of you and your friends getting wasted? How else are you supposed to remember what you did? Disposable cameras are the best option – there are some very cheap ones out there with the processing included in the price, and you don't have to spend every night out worrying if it's safe.

tv / vhs / dvd

Having a TV in your room can either turn you into a hermit or make you the most popular person on your corridor. If you like to keep yourself to yourself then an entertainment system can provide hours of solitary fulfilment. If you're the social type, inviting people to watch *Neighbours* in your room will soon turn you into 'The Host'. Don't be afraid of turfing people out when you want some alone time – your room may have turned into the new common room, but it's your room and people will respect that. But remember: televisions are not good for essay deadlines. You have been warned.

laptop / pc

When you've got one, you find you can't live without it. If you don't have one, just try not to think about it.

printer

Having a printer to accompany your computer can be a huge bonus, especially when essay deadlines all come at once and hoards of monged-out students are finishing their all-nighters with the obligatory queuing session at the only working printer in the computer lab. You will find that people start approaching you, clutching at a floppy disk with a hopeful gleam in their otherwise dull and sleep-deprived eyes. You shouldn't feel guilty for charging them.

mp3 player / walkman / cd / minidisc player / radio

Music on the go is the best way of keeping yourself entertained when trudging through the drizzle to lectures, or for drowning out the sound of the screaming child sat next to you on the bus. It's also a good way of getting mugged, but don't let that put you off. And with a pair of speakers, you can entertain yourself in your room without having to spend all your hard earned loan on a...

massive sound system

What is the point, really? You live in a tiny room surrounded by other tiny rooms divided by paper thin walls. Your music, if played at anything above a whisper, is going to be heard for miles around, so what exactly is the point of lugging all the way to university expensive equipment that has the capacity to blow the feathers off a turkey? And the time will inevitably come when someone wants to have a party, and you're the only pillock who has a 5-million-decibel sound system with copper-wired speakers. You get talked into lending it out, and then someone vomits on it. And they say they'll pay you for the damage but they never do.

before you leave home

screwdriver / tool kit

Whether it's for changing a fuse or wiring a plug, there's always someone who needs a screwdriver and there's very rarely one to be found.

guitar

OK, so you love your music, right? You live for it, yeah? There's always someone who brings their guitar, and they always become known as 'that dude with the guitar'. It's cool until it gets annoying, so think about how good you are before you pack yours.

exercise equipment

Who are you trying to kid? If you are determined to keep fit, most universities have really cheap student gyms, and local gyms often run special offers for students. And remember – jogging is free!

and now, a word from our sponsor...

To end this chapter, let's think about finances. After all, that's what this is all about, isn't it? You go to university to get the skills to get a job that will earn you lots of money. But for some reason you have to start that job whilst in thousands of pounds of debt. So, money is an issue. But with a small amount of planning before you leave home, you can carry out some foolproof preventative measures to ensure that your third year of university won't be spent trying to juggle finals revision, a dissertation, three part-time jobs and the death of your social life.

Any old fart offering advice on money will tell you to 'budget accordingly and keep a detailed record of your expenditure and income'. But are you really going to do that? Are you? Really? If it's not something you do already then it's probably not something you should start trying out when your bank account suddenly becomes a playground for loan instalments, rent payments and bills. So if you're not very good with your money (you know who you are) the key is not merely to set budgets, but to take full-on, military-style preventative measures. There's any number of ways to do this, the most obvious being to ask your parents to control your money and feed it to you as and when necessary. But it doesn't have to be that way.

The key to the foolproof financial system is damage control – you need to keep money that has to be spent on essential things like rent and bills away from your sticky mitts. A simple way of doing this is to use an instant access savings account as a holding area for all your essential outgoings, and to use your current account to hold your spending money. This way, when you do a balance check at a cash point, you have a realistic view of how much money you actually have to spend rather than a massive figure that looks very exciting but isn't really yours to play with.

With this is mind, before you start university, you should set up two bank accounts with the same bank or building society: one student account with a lovely interest free overdraft, and one instant access savings account (with a minimum deposit of £1). If your current bank doesn't provide such services, don't feel obliged to stay with them – you owe them no allegiance. It's vital that both accounts are with the same bank because you'll need to be able to transfer money instantly from one to the other. Incidentally, when you open the accounts, just ignore anything the bank might try to convince you to do. They pretend to have your interests at heart but they really, really don't. So if they offer you credit cards or any other kind of junk, stick to your guns and, in the words of Zammo Maguire, 'Just Say No'.

Draw up a list of all your expected major expenses, per term, for your first year at university. You need figures for rent, bills (although if you're living in halls this will be included in rent), TV licence (if you're taking a TV), phone bills or credit top-ups, and any miscellaneous outgoings from memberships where you pay a monthly fee (e.g. gym, insurance, etc.). And if you're super-duper organised, you might want to put aside an amount equivalent to a month's rent for a deposit on a house (as you will probably end up moving into a house in your second year and will need to pay a deposit at the same time you sign the contract).

You now have a total figure for all of your essential expenses for each term. Next, work out how much money you'll have coming in per term – student loan instalments, student grant, allowance from parents, personal savings, interest free overdraft amount (obviously if you spend any of your overdraft, it's not going to be available at the start of your next term), etc. If you subtract your total outgoings from your total income, the remaining figure is your spending money. This is what you have left to spend on books, food, clothes and partying. Disappointing, isn't it?

Because you have so little spending money, the temptation to dig into the pile that is supposed to be reserved for rent and bills can be overwhelming, particularly if all the money is just sitting there in your current account. Therefore keep as much money as possible in your instant access savings account, safe from the evil clutches of your overactive debit card. When you need to pay a bill of any kind, transfer the required amount from the savings account to your current account and pay it. If you're used to letting your direct debits happen without actually knowing how and when, you will need to start making a note of the date of these payments because it will now be your responsibility to make sure that the money is available. Because your accounts are with the same bank, the transfer will be instant and you can do it over the phone or on the Internet (provided it's over a secure connection). Meanwhile, you keep your spending money in the student current account, available for you via your debit card as and when you need it.

The amount of spending money you choose to keep in your current account is up to you. You could keep all the money that isn't needed for bills in the current account, and try to spend it slowly, or if you know that you are really bad with money, you could just keep a set budget in there, replenishing it weekly or monthly from the savings account. That way, when you hit your overdraft limit (because you spent all your allowance on beer and shoes), you'll be in trouble for a week or so, not for the whole term, or the whole year. Then, when you transfer your money the next week or the next month, you'll remember to be more careful. Plus, on the occasions when you do get overexcited and spend too much, it's a hell of a lot easier to sponge off your parents when they know on the whole you're being sensible with your money.

The fact that you have to physically transfer money from one account to another when a bill is due simply makes the whole process of spending money more tangible than just watching it disappear from your account. It forces you to think about how you spend your money, and to regularly check your financial situation so that you recognise problems early on rather than when it is too late and you have to go crying to the SU for a hardship loan.

When the first year is over, redo the whole procedure for your second year and so on. Most students get a summer job to replenish their crippled piggy bank, and this really is an excellent idea. A lot of temp agencies provide work for students over the summer, and the earlier you register the quicker they will be able to find you something. It's very unlikely that you will spend any less in your second year than you did in your first, so getting a summer job is essential if you don't want to be working during term time (this is probably the last opportunity you will ever have to live like a slob during the week, so relish it).

Well, there you have it. You're prepared, you've packed and university is just around the corner!

A slight feeling of nausea is normal at this juncture.

chapter two:

a moving experience

S tanding at the doorway of your new home, waving goodbye to the family car as it pulls mournfully out of sight, you can't help noticing that a feeling not dissimilar to that of a tiny hedgehog burrowing around your oesophagus is causing you some discomfort. In this moment of solitude your nostrils suddenly become receptive to the new smells of home. With a whiff of day-old kebabs and soggy beer mats, all at once the realisation dawns with a jerk in the pit of your stomach; this is it – you are alone. Then you turn to the stranger stood to your left and note how beautifully the tearful glimmer in their eyes enhances the words 'NEW BEST FRIEND' tattooed across their forehead. You are no longer alone...

But we're getting ahead of ourselves. While it is widely acknowledged that the most memorable moment of moving day is the sudden awareness of your new independence, the most traumatic incidents actually occur beforehand: screaming at each other in the car as your dad takes the fifth wrong turn of the journey; the near fatal embarrassment of 'Mother's Question Time' as you wait in line to collect your room key; your desperate recitation of a silent prayer in the vain hope that some divine muzzle might prevent your parents from speaking to ANYONE as you mutter awkward hellos at the people you repeatedly pass in the corridor; and the mandatory trip to the supermarket where your well-being suddenly becomes an issue for open debate and public scrutiny. But despite the disturbing nature of these most perilous of moments, the trauma is soon forgotten, just as the agony of childbirth is largely forgotten by the mother who spent fourteen hours screaming 'Please, just give me the freaking epidural, you evil bastards!'

But in the same spirit that the aforementioned mother would attend antenatal classes, it is well advised that you take measures to prepare yourself for the initial trauma of moving day, even though the associated psychological ramifications are relatively mild. You'll soon learn that the key to a smooth moving day is a focused mind and a few simple breathing techniques.

the devil makes work for idle parents

Despite what they may say, the day you leave for university is probably more difficult for your family than it is for you. While you head off to a new life of hedonism and debauchery, they are losing the precious little baby that has kept them occupied for the past eighteen years or so (unless, of course, you attended boarding school, in which case they pretty much prefer having you out of the house). With that in mind, despite the immense embarrassment they may cause you on this most stressful of days, try to be patient and understanding. Take deep breaths. Shouting at them will only invite more attention.

It's best to keep them occupied at every opportunity. If you're queuing to get your room key, take the chance to hand your folks a map and ask them to plan a route to the nearest supermarket. Once you've unloaded the car, your parents might insist on helping you unpack. If the thought of them rifling through your personal belongings is somewhat disconcerting, don't say, 'No, it's fine, I don't need any help,' because that may result in the opposite effect. Assign them a box or an area, then, while they are distracted, slip anything you might not want them getting their sticky paws on under your bed. Provided they're willing to take the bait, assigning tasks is a great way of keeping the family occupied whilst simultaneously

43

speeding up the unpacking process. Ideal distraction tasks include making the bed, setting up electronic equipment (stereo, PC, television, etc.), cleaning windows and stocking bookshelves. While they're merrily occupied, you're free to get on with a bit of...

preliminary reconnaissance

At this early stage it is vital that you take some measures to ensure that you're fully prepared for the forthcoming trip to the supermarket. Whether you've planned a big family excursion or you want to go with some new friends in the next couple of days, it's essential that you know exactly how much storage space is available before you actually commit to buying anything. Going food shopping without prior knowledge of the available storage space is a bit like trying to cram an entire pack of Hobnobs into your mouth in one go – it seemed like a good idea at the time but in fact it didn't all fit and in the end it made you throw up.

In other words, do your research before you shop. Begin in the kitchen – check out the cupboard space – how many people are sharing your kitchen? If you're not sure, check out how many rooms there are on your corridor compared with the number of kitchens. Do you have a decent amount of storage space in the kitchen? Are there lockable cupboards?

How big is the fridge? How big is the freezer? How far is the distance from your room to the kitchen? These are all factors that need to be considered when choosing your quantities for purchase. Then check out the storage space in your room – once you've unpacked all your junk will there be any extra room for kitchen stuff?

Once you have a good idea of how much space you have to play with, you're finally ready to make that perilous voyage to the supermarket. If your parents offer to drive you to the supermarket, accept the offer. Ideally your first supermarket trip should be one where you can stock up on everything you need without having to worry about carrying it all home. If they don't offer, kindly ask if it would be at all possible. If they say no, produce a packet of crisps attached to a label reading 'dinner' and place it sorrowfully on a plate. That should do the trick. Alternatively, ask them for taxi money and then wait until they realise that taking you themselves is probably the more sensible option.

At the supermarket, tension may form between you and a certain family member who wants their little baby to have everything they need, and who may try to take matters into their own hands. Well, if that means they're going to pay for your food then let it be so, but you still need to be clued up on what you're actually buying. If you demonstrate to the said family member your adeptness with quantities and budget, they might be more inclined to let you get on with it (and then provide the much appreciated cash dispensing services at the checkout). So, in the same spirit of anal-retentiveness that formed the basis of Chapter One, here's a frightfully patronising guide to grocery shopping. Enjoy!

the grocery buying guide: basics and variables

Stocking your cupboards efficiently is simply a matter of keeping a plentiful supply of the basics and a minimal supply of the variables. The basics, as you will see from the list below, provide the basis for any meal, and stockpiling them on the first supermarket visit is the cheapest and most resourceful way of ensuring you can feed yourself for the coming weeks. So, when shopping for basics you can take advantage of special offers like 'three for the price of two' without having to worry about eating it all before it goes off (because most basics are non-perishable). Then, when you've got all the basics, you can buy the variables (mostly fresh produce) as and when you need them whilst simultaneously supporting the local economy by shopping at local stores and markets. And the world is a happier place.

Buying a load of raw ingredients when you have no idea how to cook can be a little bit daunting, but remember that many items that you buy have cooking instructions printed on their packaging, or you can find information in recipe books, on the Internet, or even in the pages of this very book. So what's the big deal? With the following items, you'll be able to keep yourself fed with a variety of nutritious and tasty food at a much lower overall cost than buying processed food every week. And if you turn out to be a bit rubbish at cooking then you'll just have to get better at it because you spent all your money on ingredients. Harsh, but fair.

the basics

PASTA	Big bags of dried pasta are great. It's cheap and it's easy, and you can keep the big bag in your room and keep filling up a smaller bag to keep in the kitchen. And don't forget lasagne sheets – they're cheap and easy to cook for when you're feeling adventurous.
RICE	Choose one type of good quality rice that can be used for everything. Basmati rice is very versatile – it can be used to make pretty much anything including risotto and rice pudding, and it's lower in calories than regular long grain rice (and it tastes nicer).
COUSCOUS	Versatile, easy to prepare and fun to say out loud.

NOODLES	A big pack of egg noodles is much better value than packs of instant noodle crap, and you can choose how to flavour them with fresh ingredients or even just a stock cube rather than some nasty processed powder.
BREAKFAST CEREAL	It really is a great way to start the day – a minimum fuss food that's good for you and doesn't go mouldy, unlike bread.
STOCK CUBES	Probably the most important ingredient in the student kitchen. You should always have a good pile of stock cubes – chicken, beef, vegetable, whatever. A stock pile, if you will (oh dear).
CURRY PASTE	Why spend well over a pound on a jar of ready-made curry sauce that's way too big for one person, when you can spend fewer pennies on a jar of curry paste that can make up to ten curries as and when you are ready to eat them?
BAKED BEANS	It's a cliché, but they are great.

TINNED TOMATOES	The things you can do with a tinned tomato. Pasta sauce, salsa, curry… oh, the possibilities are endless. Plus it's cheaper than buying jars of ready-made sauces and there are fewer additives, preservatives and all those other nasty things it's fashionable to get upset about these days.
TINNED FRUIT	In juice, not syrup. Great for when scurvy is setting in and you just can't be arsed to go to the shops.
TINNED FISH	Tuna, mackerel, sardines, it's all good. Lots of Omega 3 for keeping your brain well oiled.
FROZEN VEG	Better than tinned vegetables but not as good as fresh ones. It's unlikely that you'll have much space in your freezer, so if you do want to buy some frozen vegetables get a bag of mixed ones. Or just some frozen peas – they squish into tight spots!
OIL	Vegetable, sunflower, olive, sesame – whatever takes your fancy.

CORNFLOUR	Good for thickening up sauces and it's absurdly cheap.
SUGAR	If you buy caster sugar, you can use it for baking as well as sweetening tea or coffee.
SALT	You're going to be cooking fresh food so you do actually need some!
PEPPER	Because the salt would be lonely without it.
WHITE VINEGAR	Or distilled vinegar, because it cleans windows too!
DRIED HERBS	You're not going to stock up an entire spice rack, but having the odd herb to hand makes everything taste a little more interesting. Basil is a good one, as is thyme. Mint is good for salad dressings and for making minty yoghurt dips.
CHILLI POWDER	Or Tabasco sauce. For spicing up your life.
TOMATO PUREE	For cheap pizza and pasta sauces.

PRESERVES	Peanut butter, jam, Marmite – whatever suits your loaf, so to speak.
TEA	Because it's your right as a British citizen to drink fourteen cups per day, and if the government doesn't like it, they can just pry the mug from your cold, dead hand.
COFFEE	5,000-word essay due in tomorrow? Black with two sugars please.

and you might need some...

WASHING-UP LIQUID	Must be concentrated. Avoid the really cheap stuff because it's rubbish. This is really the only cleaning fluid you need because it cleans EVERYTHING. Apart from clothes, for which you will need...
DETERGENT AND FABRIC SOFTENER	If you're a bit new to this business of washing clothes, rest assured that there's enough information printed on detergent packaging, clothing labels, the Internet and even on the walls of the laundry room for you to piece together the key steps. Or you could just ask Mummy for advice.

STAIN REMOVER	For when you spill your tea on the carpet. Or vomit.
KITCHEN ROLL	See above.
TIN FOIL	Because you're worth it.
SANDWICH BAGS	An absolute must if you're going to fit all your food in the freezer.

the variables

This is the type of stuff you should expect to be buying on a regular basis, depending on what you plan to cook. Most are also perishable, hence the reason you should buy in small quantities. You should buy variables from local stores and markets as and when you need them.

MILK	
BREAD	
BUTTER / MARGARINE / SOMETHING CLAIMING TO BE A 'SPREAD'	
EGGS	
CHEESE	
YOGHURT	
FRESH MEAT / FISH	Check out the next chapter for tips on freezer storage.

FRESH FRUIT	Never, ever buy more than five pieces of fruit at one time. Seven if you're particularly fond of fruit, but unless you're a total fruit freak it'll just go mouldy – there's only a certain amount of fruit a person can eat in one week. Always buy loose because it's so much cheaper, and if you want a variety of fruits there's nothing wrong with buying one of each.
FRESH VEGETABLES	Again, don't buy in bulk because it will only go mouldy. Especially potatoes. For some reason people feel compelled to buy giant bags of potatoes which ultimately spawn new life while they sit festering in a darkened corner of some godforsaken cupboard. Buy loose and buy as and when you need it. Although, remember – always have an onion in the cupboard.
EMERGENCY SNACK	For when it all goes a bit wrong. Sometimes cooking can defeat you – it's all part of the learning process. But it's a good idea to have a naughty little snack stashed away somewhere in case of such emergencies, to tide you over while you try to repair the damage. Otherwise, you might find yourself desperately food-napping from other people's cupboards, which will inevitably result in an onslaught of finger-wagging and bottom spanking.

Note: this list is by no means exhaustive. It contains, for example, no mention of soft drinks. That's because the list spoonfeeds you enough without telling you how and when to buy your orange juice and lemonade. Besides, you're a student; you should be drinking council pop. It's free and it comes out of the tap.

For those of you with certain food allergies or intolerances, I'm guessing if you're already aware of the ins and outs of your particular allergy / intolerance then you'll probably know which items to omit and how to substitute them. If you can't eat certain foods because of religious or moral beliefs, then you too are probably aware of what to do. If, on the other hand, you're just a fussy eater, grow up and get over it.

quoth the raven, 'that's, like, totally mingin', innit. where's the chips and that?'

Perhaps this shopping list surprises you. Perhaps you had something more along the lines of frozen pizza and chips in mind. There's no reason why you can't buy any of that stuff, of course, but there are reasons, very good reasons, why you shouldn't.

Picture the scene: you're about halfway through your first year. So far you've been living on a diet of cheese sandwiches, frozen processed delights, regular take-aways and the odd curry from a jar. Your fruit intake is derived largely from Haribo sweets and cans of Tango. And it's completely crazy, but for some reason you caught freshers' flu (formerly known as 'a cold') in the first term and you've never really shaken it off. So you're snotty all the time and your joints ache and your throat hurts. You're sleepy for most of the day, so at the age of 19 you have to take naps in the afternoon like an old git. And it would all be all right – you could deal with the bad skin, the snotty nose and tiredness – if you weren't also becoming seriously stressed out with the ever increasing pit of doom that is your overdraft; it seems that some idiot keeps spending all your money on large quantities of alcohol, junk food and toilet paper (I'll leave the reason behind the toilet paper to your imagination). That idiot is you. It's a shame; you could really do with some spare cash because you need to buy a new pair of jeans since your increasingly fat arse doesn't fit in the old ones any more.

According to a recent survey by the Unite Group, participating in sport or exercise is as favourable an activity amongst students as going to the pub, which has apparently seen a fall in popularity. But that doesn't necessarily suggest that a balanced diet is at the top of

Joe Student's agenda – four bags of crisps and a can of Coke for lunch, followed by thirty minutes on the treadmill and then a heavy night of vodka saturation in a cheesy nightclub is still consistent with Unite Group's statistic. The old saying is true – stupid is what stupid eats (or something like that). But it is also true that we, as a nation, are becoming more mindful of nutrition, thanks to the remarkable efforts of individuals such as Jamie Oliver and Captain Birds Eye.

The fact is, eating a balanced diet is good for you; it always has been and it always will be. Unfortunately, this means you have to learn how to cook using fresh ingredients. But, and this is a big but, there's no reason why you can't also enjoy the odd take-away, chocolate bar or drunken night of revelry, provided it's on a background of normal, sane eating habits, because otherwise life would be dull.

A good diet, according to the department of health, is all about variety. You can't expect to become invincible from eating fourteen oranges a day (or fourteen vitamin C supplements) because the benefits of eating fresh fruit and vegetables stem not just from their individual nutritional elements (vitamins, minerals, etc.), but also from the interactions between those elements. In other words, saturating your body with one vitamin type doesn't have the same effect as eating a variety of fresh fruit and vegetables.

What's more, the benefits of a healthy, balanced diet don't just stop at general well-being. The B-complex vitamins,

C vitamins, iron and zinc in fresh fruit and vegetables all play an important role in brain performance. Not just in improving concentration, but also in the production of hormones such as serotonin. According to a report in the *Observer* back in 2004, so many people are now on Prozac (the antidepressant that encourages serotonin production) that traces of it can actually be found in our drinking water. So if you're feeling low, think carefully about how your diet could be contributing to your mood swings before you start popping pills.

If you're still not convinced, think about it this way: when World War Three comes there'll be no frozen food and no Papa John's and we'll all have to become self-sufficient, and you'll starve to death. And then won't you feel silly.

If you're a smoker, you already know the health risks. You don't need any more people telling you 'Smoking's bad, nkay?' because you already know and you clearly aren't bothered. But, regardless of the health risks, think of the financial burden you're putting on yourself as a student. A packet of 20 cigarettes costs around five pounds. If you smoke five per day, that's one pack every four days. That's £8.75 per week. That's £455 per year. That's a considerable chunk of a non-income assessed loan (around £3,300 at time of printing) which would be enough to buy yourself a new computer or a holiday. So you end up smoking roll-ups, right? Well done you, you're getting cancer the cheap way. Applause all round.

time to say goodbye

So, once you've done all the shopping and you're feeling suitably smug for having bought so much yummy goodness, it's usually a good idea to try to get rid of your parents. They should be pretty happy knowing that you've got food and a freshly made bed, which means they should be fairly easy to shift. If they are being difficult, given that moving day is often on a Sunday you can remind them that they'll miss *Antiques Roadshow* if they don't get going soon. If all else fails just resort to brute force – they'll forgive you eventually. Then it's goodbye hugs all round, and all of a sudden you are alone...

And now we're back to where we started. The most traumatic part is over – now you're onto phase two of the unpacking process. It's sort of like ripping off a plaster; the quicker you do it, the quicker it's over, but you might lose a small amount of hair. Read on.

03:00hrs. The razor wire is in place, the bear traps are set. The beer is safe..... but for how long?

pre-emptive manoeuvres

your parents have gone and left you on your little lonesome, you're half unpacked and you've finally remembered that it's freshers' week. Suddenly, the last thing on your mind is unpacking. You want to go out and drink until your arse falls off. Well, yes, OK, do that, although the behavioural ramifications and health risks of binge drinking are a constant subject of media scrutiny, rendering the 'youth of today' as both a national embarrassment and a burden on the NHS, but if you are going to pander to the stereotype, be sure to drink lots of water in the morning. Anyway, if you do want to make your life a little easier in the coming weeks, follow the rules in this chapter as you unpack and happiness will be your reward.

Unpacking can be a right royal pain in the arse if you don't deal with it swiftly. The faster you get unpacked, the sooner you'll settle in and start to feel at home. Your room needs to look and feel like your room as soon as possible, because nothing encourages a bout of homesickness more than the sight of ugly, bare walls and a bulging suitcase in the corner. With that in mind, be sure to get the important tasks over and done with first. Start by making your bed (although, if you were paying attention in the last chapter this would have already been done for you), then at least if you give up early you've got something in which to sleep. Next, get some posters or photos up on the walls and instantly the room seems a little more like your own. There's usually a rule specifying that the use of Blu Tack on the walls is 'strictly prohibited', but it often seems like a strange rule when the walls are already covered in Blu Tack stains. (Incidentally, take a look at Chapter Seven for tips on Blu Tack stain removal.)

Unpacking your food and kitchenware, on the other hand, carries a slightly higher degree of urgency. Where the kitchen is concerned you need to mark your territory as early as possible; the first few days of term are a transitional period for the kitchen, since there will be very few people confident enough to behave in the manner to which they will stoop in the weeks to come (some people won't even be confident enough to eat, let alone cook, in public). Your preliminary reconnaissance should have allowed you to shop accordingly, so now is the time to carry out some pre-emptive manoeuvres. Or, to put it simply, it's time to unpack the shopping!

storage:
a tripartite solution

The rules are simple. There are three categories of storage for food and kitchenware:

1) Bedroom storage (the safe haven)

2) Kitchen storage (the danger zone)

3) Fridge/freezer storage (an unavoidable but risky business)

categories I and II:
decisions and consequences

Fundamentally, your bedroom, with its lockable door and distinction of privacy, is a safe haven for your most treasured possessions. It makes sense to assume that anything kept in there, as opposed to in the kitchen, will be safe from those pilfering pixies. And rest assured that if anyone were to break in to your bedroom, they would be far more likely the student kitchen survival handbook

to steal your TV and your iPod than your beloved wok. Phew!

Precisely which items of food or kitchenware you decide to store in your bedroom and which to store in the kitchen is, therefore, a personal decision. But that decision can also be influenced by the particulars of each room available to you. For instance, you might not have any storage space in your bedroom, you might not have any storage space in the kitchen, or, conversely, you might be really lucky and have lockable storage space in the kitchen. Anyway, herein shall be a more detailed argument for keeping as much as possible out of the kitchen.

pots and pans

Keeping pots and pans in the bedroom sounds like a right pain in the arse. But think about it; these are the most annoying things to clean, especially when somebody else has used them because they couldn't be bothered to clean their own. Perhaps you left your clean saucepan in the kitchen for the taking and now it has day-old tuna mayonnaise welded to its sides. Equally, a clean saucepan in a kitchen in which the dirty crockery has reached critical mass can and will be commandeered as a drinking receptacle or cereal bowl. And don't expect anything non-stick to stay that way. Leaving pots and pans in the kitchen is a death sentence for Teflon. First come the little scratches, then someone uses a knife to scrape off the four-day-old egg fused to the base

– next thing you know, there are little black flakes in your omelette.

cooking utensils (spatula, wooden spoon, etc.)

Again, keeping these in your room has its benefits, namely that you can monitor where they are. If you leave them in the kitchen they will get used, especially if they are the only ones there. These are also likely to get damaged, melted, set on fire or used to unblock toilets. You have been warned.

small appliances

We have already explored the reasons why you don't really need to bring these with you, but some people start to hyperventilate when more than four feet away from a kettle at any given time, so you might have brought one regardless. Most accommodation offices will stipulate that you must not use any small appliances, such as kettles or toasters, in your bedroom. This is not a recommendation that you break that rule, but if you don't want them to become available for general use (or abuse), it would be wise to keep any such appliance in your bedroom and take it to the kitchen as and when is necessary.

The one item you should really keep out of the kitchen is a toasted sandwich maker. Students LOVE them and will use them incessantly without cleaning, rendering them sticky and gross in a matter of days.

crockery and cutlery

These will disappear if you leave them in the kitchen. However, if you followed the rules of buying and these items are monstrous enough to stand out from the rest, then they should be easy enough to retrieve.

sauces, seasoning, stock cubes and herbs

On a scale of 1 to 'goodbye', these items are off the chart when it comes to the risk of being used or stolen. Leave a student a jar of dried basil on the worktop and he will eat for one day, but give him the tools and seeds he needs to grow his own and he will tell you to 'piss right off' because he'd rather get it the easy way. To put it simply, if there's stuff lying around that will make somebody's hideous concoction taste better, they will use it. Everybody does it. Everybody.

non-refrigerated food (e.g. pasta, tins, etc.)

If there's one thing that's worse than people using your pots and pans it's people nicking your food. It can and does happen. It is in fact theft, and if it happens often then you should report it to the appropriate accommodation authorities who will no doubt issue a very scary letter of warning to the suspected culprits who will be too stoned to care.

cleaning products

Actually, there really is little danger in keeping these in a cupboard in the kitchen. The worst thing that could happen is someone uses them to do some cleaning. It's probably a bad idea to leave washing-up liquid out on view, though – people who are new to the whole washing-up phenomenon tend to think that washing-up liquid needs to be administered in equal proportions to water.

To sum up categories 1 and 2, just bear in mind that anything you leave in the kitchen ultimately becomes public property. You can put your name on it, you can sprinkle it with your own urine, but short of sticking it in a bear trap, there's nothing you can do to stop some bastard from using it. So if it's yours and yours alone, keep it in your room. That said, you might actually be the kind of person who doesn't mind people using your stuff in the kitchen. (There was even a time when I was the generous sort. Sharing is caring, after all. But that was a long time ago. The ravages of experience have left me old and embittered...)

category III:
fridge and freezer storage

Chilled food is such a contradiction in terms. There is nothing 'chilled' about fridge and freezer storage. Bear in mind that with the fridge and the freezer, establishing your space on the first day should be carried out with a sense of urgency.

These areas get full very quickly, and if you don't act with haste you might end up shoving your courgettes between someone else's yoghurt pots. And, to reiterate the sentiment of the previous chapter, don't buy more than you can fit in what little space you have. It's unfair on other people. And remember that most fruit doesn't need to be refrigerated, and a fruit bowl in your room will actually look quite nice.

the inevitability of theft

People will pinch milk. They will pinch butter. They may even steal cheese. Precious cheese! *You* will even commit these atrocities from time to time, as an act of utter desperation, of course. But you can give yourself a hand by following the rules of size-based ethics. The psychology of it is simple;

the more you buy, the more people are likely to steal. Don't piss people off by buying an enormous family-sized tub of margarine: it takes up space and people will just steal from it. Buy a smaller tub and then the theft of a bit of spread is more noticeable, therefore it is less likely to happen.

On the other hand, by buying small you are increasing the rate at which your food supply will diminish, thus making you more inclined to steal because you can't be bothered to go to the shops. Isn't life unfair? The ultimate solution is to find a buddy with whom to share items such as milk and butter. You can buy bigger but ultimately take up less room in the fridge. And it's cheaper!

fridge tips

bag it

If you are keeping fruit or vegetables in the fridge, make sure you keep them in bags. While it is true that this causes them to perish more quickly, a whole range of nasty surprises can and will breed in a communal fridge, and it's best to keep your produce protected. Pierce the bags to let the fruit and veg breathe.

Sometimes certain things won't fit in the fridge. For instance, if you buy a whole cabbage, lettuce, broccoli or cauliflower, more often than not they're just a bit too big and round to fit in the shelf space. There are two ways to get around this: either slice them down the middle and stick the two halves in separately, or break the leaves (or florets) apart and keep them in a bag.

cans in the fridge

Please, for the love of God, don't keep opened cans in the fridge. Leaving food in an open can allows the metal inside to oxidise and transfer into the food, especially if the contents are particularly acidic (like fruit, for example). The food in the can ends up tasting gross and it's really not good for you. But more than that, cans tend to get knocked over in the fridge, and putting a pissy bit of cling film over the top will not stop all the mouldy beans from oozing out everywhere. So if you are saving surplus food from an open can, put it in some Tupperware and recycle the can! And then forget about the Tupperware and find it a month later as its contents try to climb out of the fridge of their own accord.

If you are defrosting meat in the fridge, put it on the very bottom shelf so that those nasty salmonella juices can't drip onto anything below. And finally, to avoid a build-up of icky sminge at the bottom of the fridge drawers, line them with a sheet or two of kitchen roll.

freezer tips

There is likely to be little space for you to store anything in the freezer, especially as time goes on and the layer of ice coating the sides begins to resemble some sort of yeti enclosure. The best thing you can do is to put everything you buy into individual sandwich or freezer bags. For instance, if you buy a pack of four chicken fillets, open it and put each fillet in a separate bag. That way you can squish them all in to a tighter spot in the freezer, and you won't have to break them apart when you want to cook them. The same rule can apply to things that come in boxes like waffles and mini pizzas – ditch the box and save the space, although be sure to keep the cooking instructions from the box or you might be in a bit of a pickle when it comes to cooking them. Obviously things in bags should remain in the bag, like frozen vegetables and chips. Just try not to buy enormous bags of these items because it will only end in defrosted tears.

a short note about labels

This extends to all categories of storage, not just the fridge. Some people feel compelled to stick their name on everything they own. This will often work in the respect that any would-be thief would rather pinch food from a random victim as opposed to a named one (it's easier to bear the guilt that way). However, labelling all your food may sometimes get yourself labelled as an anal twat. It's your call. Some people find it useful to mark their food packages with a dot from a marker pen to distinguish their items from those of other people, and then to keep a secret inventory of everything purchased. That way, you know exactly what you own and you're not jibing anyone's turkey. And if you can't be arsed to write a list, just use your shopping receipt. Genius!

'I'm not a freak, honest'

After hearing the mysterious shuffling noises coming from your bedroom, seeing you run back and forth from your room to the kitchen with armfuls of junk and witnessing the odd moment in which you have sat crouched on the floor, stroking a tin of beans whilst croaking the words 'my precious' over and over again, your housemates might start to think you're a bit of a nut job. You might also find that you twitch uncontrollably whenever anyone is within a foot of your cupboard. That's OK, you're probably just suffering from a small degree of paranoia that may or may not have developed from reading this book. Not to worry, though, proving you're not a maniac should be pretty straightforward, provided, of course, that you aren't actually a maniac. Students are fickle little monkeys, so buying their love is easy – produce a big box of chocolates or a giant pizza for everyone to share, or if you're good at cooking, make a big meal. Your erratic behaviour will soon be forgotten, plus it's a lovely thing to do and it will bring you all closer together. And then while they're distracted you can gather up all your food and bury it in a giant pit where they'll never find it! Mwah ha ha ha haaa!

Note: please don't bury your food in a pit. And if you are a maniac please seek professional help.

pre-emptive manoeuvres

Now you've prepared yourself for what lies ahead, go out and party. Your food is safe and, mild paranoia aside, you should be stress free. And when you get hungry, read the next chapter.

chapter four:

and we're cooking

picture the scene: it's 5 p.m. and you've just spent the entire day finding new and interesting ways of procrastinating before you make a start on the assignment that's due in tomorrow morning. Maybe you and your friends made a series of forts and communicated with each other through telephones made from paper cups and string. Maybe you spent four hours debating whether or not the series of events in the original *Star Wars* trilogy can, in fact, all be attributed to the actions of one seemingly inconsequential gunner on the *Star Destroyer* at the beginning of the first film. Maybe you created a mythical kingdom of toilet rolls ruled by a hierarchical body of differently sized Marmite pots, each adorned with a tinfoil crown and sceptre.

Either way, it's all hard work. And now you are hungry and have a long night of hard graft ahead of you. So you amble into the kitchen to whip up some brain food for the arduous task ahead – but, no! There is no kitchen! What was once the kitchen has been replaced by a ceramic battlefield, bathed in the stench of death and littered with the gruesome vestiges of the Great Crockery War! Fallen plates lie in moribund piles, encrusted with the decaying stains of combat. Forked and serrated weaponry is strewn about the battlefield, still caked in the entrails of it's victims…

… Or, the kitchen is quite messy because no lazy sod has bothered to wash up in a while. Now, it's difficult to say when the kitchen will get into this state. It might take days, it might even take weeks, but at some point it will turn into a shit pit. It's inevitable. What's important is that you learn how to feed yourself in such circumstances, because getting all riled up and shouting obscenities isn't going to get you anywhere on an empty stomach.

first things first:
create a workspace

We are operating under the assumption that you are aiming to cook real food here. If it's simply a matter of bunging some frozen nuggets of processed beaks and bumholes into the oven for twenty minutes, then all you need to do is find a clean oven tray. Good luck. But if there's some serious and tasty cooking about to take place, the first thing you will need to do is create a clean work surface. This might seem like a slightly depressing prospect if the mess facing you was wholly unexpected, but it can be relatively painless if dealt with appropriately.

You might only want to commandeer a small area of work surface, or you may need to use the whole kitchen for the meal you've got planned, but whatever the situation, don't worry about washing the mounds of crap standing between you and your next culinary adventure. If it isn't your mess then it isn't your problem. So, put on your rubber gloves (you don't have to, it just makes the whole ordeal a little less traumatic) and take all the dirty crockery, cutlery and kitchenware that is littering the area you need to be clear (including stuff filling the sink and on top of the oven) and pile it all up in one place.

At times, particularly if you haven't been into the kitchen for a while, you will need to be prepared for some of these items to be nothing short of vomit-inducing. If you're lucky, you might stumble upon a forgotten saucepan filled with what used to be baked beans but what is now a living, breathing organism soon to be hell-bent on world domination (otherwise known as mould). You might even find yourself faced with a chopping board complete with decorative slivers of day-old raw chicken. Hence the rubber gloves. But however unpleasant the situation, don't do anybody's work for them, just stick everything in your chosen spot, regardless of its state. Just remember: you are here to cook, not wipe the arse of humanity.

That said, NEVER pile everything into the sink. This is a death sentence for dishes. Once they are piled into the sink they will not be washed. Apart from the fact you can't use the sink for anything else if it's full, the sight of dishes sitting in the sink triggers an impulse in the student brain that subconsciously guides the subject into the misapprehension that somehow those dishes will magically clean themselves, like they do back home when Mummy is around. Plus, when someone is finally brave enough to take them out of the sink and wash them, they will be faced with unspeakable things that will have cultivated in the damp conditions.

Oh, and don't pile everything in front of the microwave either because that's a really stupid thing to do. The door opens outwards, you know.

You should now have a work surface that is cleared of junk. Next you should quickly use a sponge or cloth with a bit of warm water and washing-up liquid to clean it and wipe away any encrusted gunk. Yes, that did sound a bit patronising. Sorry. Now, if you have been assiduous enough to stay on top of your washing-up and you've been keeping crockery and kitchenware in your bedroom, you won't have to worry about finding the appropriate items to clean in all the mess. You can fetch the things you need to cook with, do what you have to do, wash up when you're done, put everything back in your room and life will be a slice of pie.

If you don't keep your belongings out of the kitchen, then you're going to have to dig through the mounds of crap to find something to wash, and that procedure takes a hell of a lot longer. Annoying, isn't it?

bollocks to that, I just want to eat

Sometimes, you just can't be bothered to clear up other people's filth. Hell, sometimes you can't be arsed to clean your own filth! But not to worry, there are many delicious meals that can be made using only the cooking receptacle as the preparation area. And that doesn't just include frozen junk and ready-meals, although these can provide a solution in times of absolute desperation. But if you wish to cook something that will keep you full for more than a nano-second and not clog your arteries with icky goo, then you could ditch the chopping board and come up with some more imaginative ways of preparing your ingredients.

chopping without a chopping board

Scissors are a much-overlooked item of kitchenware, over-shadowed by the glamorous kitchen knife. Yes, the knife has the body, the looks and that element of mystery and danger, but scissors are safe, practical and less likely to hurt you in the long run. You can use scissors to chop almost any cut of meat (provided it's been defrosted) and a whole variety of vegetables such as cabbage, green beans, any fresh herb and lettuce (although really you should tear lettuce with your hands, apparently). Simply hold the item in one hand over the cooking receptacle or serving dish and snip away with the other. Broccoli and cauliflower can also be prepared in this way – just snip off the florets at the stem.

Some items, however, do have to be cut with a sexy knife on a not so sexy chopping board; scissors tend to fail when confronted with onions, leeks, potatoes and turnips. But there are a number of items that can be chopped with a knife without using a flat surface as a base. This is not by any means a safe or particularly practical thing to do, and you are absolutely not recommended to do it, but it's a technique with which you should be familiar for theoretical purposes. If, say, you weren't in the mood to dig out a chopping board, you could hold the item of food in one hand, and with the other hand slice it with a sharp knife by applying pressure to the back of the blade with the side of your forefinger, slicing towards you and stopping the blade with your thumb once it has cut through. The slice falls neatly into the cooking receptacle or dish. This method works like a treat for soft items such as cucumbers, courgettes, celery, tomatoes, apples, bananas and cheese but don't risk it with any hard vegetables or it could end in tears.

Bear in mind that if you are chopping over the cooking receptacle, it might be a good idea to take it off the heat while you are doing so. For instance, if you're making a chicken stir-fry and you're busy chopping peppers into the pan while it's still on the heat, then you might be eating a chargrilled chicken stir-fry by the time you're finished.

steaming without a steamer

Fill a pan with a small amount of water and put over the hob. Cover with a lid until it boils (i.e. steam is coming off it). Meanwhile, put your vegetables in a metal sieve. When the water is boiling, place the sieve inside the pan, hooking it on the side so the bottom of the sieve isn't touching the water. Then rest the lid over the whole lot and leave it for a while. After four minutes or so, stick a fork in to test the texture and the temperature. When you feel it's ready, eat it.

minimalist mess

There are hundreds of ways in which you can make tasty and nutritious food while minimising the number of items that become dirty in the process. You just need to use your initiative. For instance, when cooking on the hob for one, you should never have to use more than two pots or pans for a meal. If you are boiling vegetables, boil them together. If they have different boiling times, put the ones that take the longest in first and then add the rest accordingly. When they're ready, you can avoid the use of a colander by spooning them out of the water with a straining spoon or using a fork. If you're frying food, fry it all in the same pan. It all sounds ridiculously simple but you wouldn't believe the number of people who insist on using a different receptacle for each item of food.

yesterday's dinner is today's lunch

Leftovers, if handled properly, are great. When cooking at night, always make enough for leftovers – it minimises your cooking time. Don't do it with lunch and dinner on the same day because you'll get sick of eating the same thing, but make too much for dinner in the evening and then have it for lunch or dinner the next day. The best way of storing leftovers is in a plastic container in the fridge. But be sure to wait until the food has cooled before you seal the box and put it in the fridge, otherwise terrible things will happen. Terrible things.

cooking from an empty cupboard

Sometimes you will find that you don't appear to have any food but you are very hungry and the prospect of going to the shop to buy something has you reaching for the take-away menus despite the fact that you haven't got the money to be ordering out. In these instances, use your imagination. The fundamental rules of cooking are simple. Start with a base – pasta, bread, couscous, rice, whatever. Then look at what you have in your cupboard. A tin of tomatoes? A beef stock cube? Mix with some herbs and you've got a delicious pasta sauce. Any meat will go with it, or pretty much any type of vegetable. Just try to imagine the taste of a foodstuff, and then think of how it would taste paired with something else. (An old favourite in my house was chicken kiev with noodles and pesto, green beans and mayonnaise. Sounds disgusting but it was delicious and filling.) Be experimental, but don't go crazy. Some things will not work together and will only make you ill. For instance, pickled onions and milk is a bit of a no-no. Use your common sense. As a university student you must be oozing with the stuff.

the magic of stock cubes

Stock cubes, either meat or vegetable, make everything taste good. If you are completely hard up, noodles boiled with a stock cube will feed you. Pasta boiled with a stock cube will feed you. Even rice boiled with a stock cube will feed you and it's all a damn sight cheaper than buying one of those packs of processed noodle poo. Be aware that there are many brands of stock cube available, and if you are going to buy the economy ones then try not to eat anything cooked with a better quality stock cube because you'll notice the difference.

the cooking buddy

The one thing that prevents most people from taking the time to prepare a good meal is the dissatisfaction and general feeling of emptiness that can be associated with cooking for one. It's a depressing business, and often seems like a waste of time. So if you can, find yourself a cooking buddy. When there are two people on the job, cooking becomes a social activity rather than a chore. You can make things that you both enjoy and you can split the workload. And there's no reason why you have to shop together, you could just cook some of your food one day and some of theirs the next. Having a cooking buddy can even make the most stressful of kitchen conditions more bearable. You might even find yourself joking about it. 'Ha ha! Look at the mould on my frying pan.'

worst case scenario

Although cooking is essentially very easy, there are some risks involved. The absolute worst thing that can happen is that you give yourself food poisoning. No, wait, scratch that. The worst thing that can happen is that you set fire to the house. Either way, it may result in death. But provided you take a few very simple precautions, you should live to cook another day. It seems ironic considering the context of your mould ridden kitchen, but hygiene is a huge issue, especially where raw meat is concerned. Always wash your hands after handling RAW MEAT, always wash your scissors or your knife after cutting RAW MEAT, and never use the same implement to chop vegetables if it hasn't been washed after touching RAW MEAT. RAW MEAT bad, soap and water good.

When cooking meat, make sure it is piping hot all the way through. That means that when you cut it open, it's very hot inside, it all looks the same colour (i.e. not pink), the juices run clear and there is steam coming off it.

Finally, always keep an eye on anything that is cooking under the grill or on the hob, because flambé is best left to the professionals. Sober professionals. (Yes, a big fat chip buttie might have seemed like a good idea when you staggered in drunk at 3 a.m., but when the fire alarm starts wailing after you've passed out on the sofa, nobody else in your building seems to agree…)

just use your noodle

So much of what happens in the kitchen is all down to common sense. Cooking can be a joy if you allow yourself to relax and to experiment. And now you have the skills and the knowledge to survive in the vilest of kitchens, you can finally start cooking those delicious recipes from your favourite cookbook! And you're still sane and forming coherent sentences. Good for you!

and we're cooking

Now you have fed yourself, you can start dealing with the horrid children that made all this mess in the first place. And you should probably make a start on that assignment too...

chapter five:

kitchen politics

t o introduce the complex subject that is 'kitchen politics', let us turn to the greatest philosopher that never existed, Fydo Küchegaard, in an extract from his acclaimed work; *The Existential Kitchen*:

Through the development of familiarity between student and student, and between student and kitchen appliance, the mere act of feeding oneself in the kitchen and the social interactions that occur therein become increasingly effortless. After the total familiarisation of appliance functionality, the wandering student mind begins to explore more deeply the environment in which its food is prepared, and how the complex interplay of body, flame, spoon, grease residue and countless other variables affect the self. 'Who am I? Why do I exist? What differentiates me from the spoon? Why must I wash the spoon?' In the context of atmospheric relaxation as a consequence of the developing student–student familiarity dynamic, the student determines answers to these questions through simple experimentation and an assessment of the consequences (washing the spoon / not washing the spoon; possessing a clean spoon / incitement of malevolence). Therefore, while the student–kitchen relationship remains entirely objective, the method of attaining the objective becomes subjective. The manner in which the student decides to fulfil the objective (to feed oneself) thus forms the essence of the student, and consequently the dynamic of the student–student relationship is inevitably altered. Fundamentally, it is only through the incremental growth of familiarity between student and student that the essence of the student can truly develop.

We surmise, therefore, that a tidy kitchen is an unfamiliar kitchen.

Yes, it really doesn't take a genius to point out that as you begin to ease into a more comfortable social routine with your new housemates, the state of the kitchen inevitably changes. Regardless of whether or not you actually like your housemates, you will begin to feel more relaxed from having spent every waking moment in each other's near vicinity (and from hearing each other pass wind for the first time) which begins to turn people who were, in the beginning, a little more nervous about leaving a mess in the kitchen into filthy slobs. In light of this changing atmosphere, with time you may notice that certain people (yourself included) begin to fall into a range of stereotypical behavioural categories. Here's an insight into some of the more common kitchen personalities you might come across:

kitchen victim

typical attributes:

Constantly furrowed brow, trembling bottom lip and clothing spattered with dirt. If you squint, above the head of a true kitchen victim you might catch a glimmer of a little ketchup-stained halo.

general description:

Every day is a struggle for the kitchen victim. They want only for a simple life; a life in which they can prepare the occasional meal in a tidy and hygienic kitchen, wash their dishes and get on with the rest of their day. But every dirty dish, every mouldy cup and every greasy frying pan blocking this dream destroys another tiny bit of their soul. A typical kitchen victim will face early onslaughts of other people's mess returns the next day. Being a natural creature of habit, however, the kitchen victim will repeat this pattern day after day, chipping away at their own tolerance threshold until finally, one day, they simply down tools and declare: 'No more!' Thus the kitchen victim enters into a transitional period in which he or she may transform into any other kitchen personality type. More often than not they turn out to be a gobshite (see below).

eating habits:

The kitchen victim often enjoys cooking pasta dishes for large groups of people and then secretly resenting the lack of gratitude received from those for whom they toiled.

kitchen tourist

typical attributes:

Running shoes, backpack, telescopic spoon.

general description:

In the world of the kitchen tourist, a good meal is a free meal. The kitchen tourist will gleefully sail from kitchen to kitchen, using crockery, utensils and appliances as and when they find them. Well-mannered tourists will leave the kitchen in the state in which they found it, but the actions of a less respectful tourist may be tantamount to kitchen terrorism.

eating habits:

There exists a breed of parasitic kitchen tourist who will flit from kitchen victim to kitchen victim, 'selflessly' adopting any of their dinnertime leftovers. The more adept at this technique can survive for days without cooking at all.

kitchen pixie

typical attributes:

Invisible to the human eye.

general description:

The kitchen pixie is a mystical spirit that dwells in the deepest, darkest recesses of mould-ridden cupboards. Driven by an unaccountable compulsion for mischief, the invisible pixie will emerge and possess the body of the first student it comes across, forcing them to act against their will in a variety of kitchen-based misdemeanours. Once the deed is done, the pixie exits the host body, leaving the student blissfully unaware of what just occurred. Then someone finds a bite has been taken out of their block of cheese. Chaos ensues, but the culprit remains undiscovered.

eating habits:

Decidedly unpredictable.

kitchen gobshite

typical attributes:

Raised voice and wild gesticulations.

general description:

Kitchen gobshites abound in messy kitchens, and typically accompany the presence of a kitchen terrorist. Essentially, the gobshite will wax lyrical about 'the tragic state of the kitchen' without ever actually approaching the suspected culprit directly, or indeed working towards a solution. Back in the 1980s, a band of kitchen gobshites would frequent Speaker's Corner in London's Hyde Park, but recent, more apathetic times have seen the rhetoric of the gobshite descend into mere whinging to friends. That said, the most extreme of kitchen gobshites may actually go to the lengths of writing an entire book about student kitchens. Subtlety isn't really their forte.

eating habits:

The typical gobshite has a tendency to eat out, regularly.

kitchen terrorist

typical attributes:

Shifty eyes.

general description:

The kitchen terrorist will leave their plates unwashed because they believe it is their right to do so. Kitchen terrorism has often been linked with cookbook fundamentalism – a movement purporting that the cookbook should be taken literally from beginning to end (and since most cookbooks bear no mention of the washing-up process, the kitchen terrorist neglects to do so). Recent years have seen a growing number of incidents in which the kitchen gobshite has accused the kitchen terrorist of possessing kitchen utensils of mass destruction. The Students Union have taken measures to monitor such allegations, and in a radical move in 2004, NUS resolution 1540 recognised the threat posed to kitchen security by utensils of mass destruction, and called upon greater effort from kitchen gobshites, victims and tourists to limit the proliferation of such utensils. The problem continues nonetheless.

eating habits:

Food is obtained by whatever means necessary and consumption is generally uncouth.

kitchen protocol

As you can see, the state of any kitchen is dictated largely by the presence of certain personalities therein. In terms of kitchen demography, a kitchen with a high population of victims and gobshites and a low population of terrorists will remain relatively tidy. Wouldn't that be nice? In less happy circumstances (i.e. a high ratio of terrorists to victims), more often than not the state of the kitchen is inalterable and the best thing to do is get on with your life, adhering to the rules laid out in Chapter Four. There are times, however, when the desire to enforce change becomes overwhelming, like when you put your hand in a pile of goo. In such instances, there are right and wrong ways to take action, so here are a few useful tips for dealing with serious troublemakers.

DO NOT play Chinese Whispers. If there's someone causing a constant problem by not doing their share, some people instinctively gossip about the culprit without ever actually addressing them personally. This gets you nowhere.

DO NOT leave little notes. If the troublemaker is one person in particular, they will probably just get defensive and paranoid

91

because everyone got to read the note. If it's from you to a group of people, they will inevitably start making fun of you behind your back. There is a time and a place for notes but this is not one of them.

DO NOT draw up a rota. In halls, this is a really dumb idea and in a house it's a very complex issue.

DO NOT get angry about a messy kitchen if you know that a lot of the mess is your own. That's called being a hypocrite.

DO be honest. If a bunch of you have a grievance, tell the person. Sit them down and as a group explain that the mess they leave is disrespectful to everyone who has to share the kitchen (or living room / bathroom / whatever). They will retort with 'But you left a bowl of beans out for five days!' and then you'll all get into a big argument. The accused will eventually clean the kitchen, and then the normal state of affairs will resume in about a week.

DO stay calm. If you feel that you are living alone in a kitchen of dirty slobs, then, well, it doesn't look good for you. Keep a cool head. Learn to breeze on past a pile of junk rather than getting all stressed out about it. In your case, tolerance will be your saviour.

Alternatively, DO turn into a psychopath. In a really awful kitchen, turn completely psychotic every time you see a pile of dirty dishes, making sure that the culprit is in the room, or within earshot at the time. Bang stuff about, slam cupboard doors, generally go crazy, but don't direct the rage at any particular person, just the mess itself. For fear of a repeat performance, the culprit will clean up the mess and if the display was frightening enough, the effects may be lasting.

There are many ways to handle a troublemaker, but sadly, as far as long-term change is concerned, each of them is likely to fail. It's unlikely that anyone is ever going to change their lazy habits just because someone gives them a bit of a bollocking. Some people are simply disrespectful of other people's property, and it's very difficult to force individuals to change their ways. However, if someone completely trashes the kitchen (or, as mentioned before, steals a load of food), then you need to file an official complaint with the appropriate accommodations authority. Then they can deal with it in their own special way.

We've looked a little at the major troublemakers; let's take a moment to look at some of the other, minor issues that can affect well-being in the kitchen.

sud's law

There comes a time in the life of every kitchen when the washing-up gets done. These things happen quite organically. It might just start with a comment, a tiny idea, and then suddenly someone picks up a sponge and before you know it there are suds flying about as though there was no tomorrow. But, in retrospect, the process of washing-up can often seem like a bit of a waste of time. Namely because some people are very bad at it. So here are some pointers.

Basically, there's a telltale sign that the washing-up isn't working – there's sminge all over the 'clean' plates. This phenomenon stems from a British obsession with teeny, tiny washbasins. In terms of water ecology, such washbasins are essential, but you can't ignore the fact that a plate covered in bubbles on the drying rack is not a clean plate. Those bubbles contain itty bitty bits of food. These stick to the plate as it dries, or to the tea towel (making it smell icky), or they stick to the drying rack, rendering it all grimy and disgusting. So the simple solution is this: wash your plates in the sink or basin, as usual, then rinse them, just a tiny bit, to get rid of the bubbles. A rinsed plate is a clean plate. End of sermon.

mould: a social issue

You're busy rifling trough the immense pile of crockery that's been stacked by the kitchen sink for the past two weeks. You're looking for a spatula. Then you lift a pile of plates off the top of a saucepan, and inside is revealed a whole new ecosystem. There are fungus trees and fungus wildebeests and tiny little mould people running about. What to do? The initial reaction is to scream. Once this preliminary shock has passed, the best thing to do is calmly put the offending item in the centre of the room, on a table or on the floor, wherever it will attract the most attention. Then just leave it there. After it becomes the topic of a heated debate between your housemates, the culprit will feel guilty enough to clean it (in secret, of course). Alternatively, if it's still in the centre of the room after a few days, throw it away.

If the pan is yours but the mould is the product of someone having borrowed it, the likelihood is you'll know who borrowed it and you can ask them to sort it out. If, on the other hand, the pan is yours but you don't know who borrowed it... well, life's a bitch sometimes.

If the pan is yours and the mould is yours, which it might well be, the best thing to do is don your Marigolds and scoop out the mould into the bin. Squirt in some washing liquid and add really hot water. Then leave it to stand for a few hours and wash. Simple.

fridge faq

Sometimes strange things happen to the fridge. A fridge-based trauma can be a frightening and confusing experience, but never fear, the Fridge FAQ is here.

Q: our fridge is smelly. it's making everything taste bad. why is our fridge smelly and what should i do?

A: Detective work is called for here. Pull on the rubber gloves and clear out the whole fridge. You'll come across the culprit eventually. Remember to group the items according to which shelf you pulled them from because otherwise you'll put them back in the wrong places and incur the wrath of the masses.

Things that contain a lot of garlic tend to release quite potent smells that overwhelm the other foodstuffs. Look out for ageing salami sausages, old pizza, mouldy curries and elderly cloves of 'fresh' garlic. Milk or fresh juice that's leaked and is festering at the bottom of the fridge is another common stinky culprit, and rotting meat and fish tend to get a wee bit pongy too.

Q: our fridge has a pool of water at the bottom. why does our fridge have a pool of water at the bottom?

A: Either something is leaking or there's something wrong with the fridge. Get out the Marigolds and soak up the water with a sponge or kitchen roll. Check all the bottles and jars for leaks and tighten lids of suspected culprits. Then leave it for a day or so – if the liquid reappears there might be a problem with the fridge, so call maintenance (or the landlord, if you're in a house).

Q: when i put things towards the back of the fridge they freeze. why?

A: The fridge setting is on too high. Lower it slightly using the temperature or power gauge (there's one in there, you just need to look for it). The fuller the fridge, the higher the power setting has to be, so if it's not very full a high power setting will make the fridge too cold.

Q: some of my food has gone missing. where is my food?

A: Sadly, this has nothing to do with the fridge. You've either fallen victim to the work of a kitchen pixie, or some poor soul has had an attack of the dreaded munchies. Locate the culprit and avenge the death of your Mini Babybels.

So there you have it. Disappointed? You bet you are. There are no easy answers and no magic resolutions to kitchen-based problems. But that's no reason to give up the fight! C'est la vie.

part two

Staring into the mug, Stuart knew his mission: To mouldly go where no man has gone before.

life in halls is like a box of chocolates — mostly brown and likely to stain your t-shirt

et's take a moment to explore some of the other dank little corners of your university abode, because even though it may be the centre of discontent, not all deplorable student activity is confined to the kitchen — there are also shared common rooms, toilets, bathrooms and the occasional shared bedroom to consider. Remember the glossy accommodation brochure that arrived with your acceptance letter? Thumbing through its pages, your eyes would have been privy to a selection of colourful and engaging photographs of shiny-faced students enjoying their 'typical' living spaces: a semi-attractive young girl perched daintily at a solid oak desk in her minimalist boudoir; a group of familiar looking youngsters laughing heartily at a shared joke in the setting of a streamlined common room; and two bespectacled youths sitting on the grass, discussing literature against a backdrop of sunlit shrubbery. This manner of depicting student accommodation is known as 'The Hollyoaks Effect'. As you are probably already aware, the reality of student life is somewhat less refined.

The design of student accommodation shares certain features with that of nurseries and care homes, since their specifications are all relatively similar: heavy security, wipe-clean surfaces, durable furniture and a neutral colour scheme that complements bodily-fluid-based stains. If accommodation brochures captured the true image of life in halls, the semi-attractive girl would be defacing the desk with Biro doodles, the familiar looking youngsters would be laughing at their housemate lying face down in a pile of his own vomit on the common room floor, and the bespectacled youths – well, actually, they would still be sat on the grass in order to avoid the smell inside the common room. The point is, while every halls of residence or student village is different in design, the activities that occur therein are universally destructive. So, once again, it's a good idea to prepare yourself and have your wits about you.

the social scene

The halls experience is shaped by the people with whom you live rather than the design of the living space itself, not only in terms of friendships and grievances, but also in the sense that the personalities, habits and standards of personal hygiene amongst the inhabitants generally determine the condition of that living space. University admin seem to adopt a completely random selection process in deciding who will be living with whom, so there really is no way of knowing what kind of reprobate you'll have as a next-door neighbour. You might end up loving your neighbours, or you might absolutely despise them, but regardless of your feelings for each other there are a few useful tips that can work in your favour in any halls-based social situation.

hi, my name is...

You meet so many people in freshers' week, it's almost too easy to simply forget people's names the instant you are introduced. During the first week it's not a huge problem, since everybody is still getting to know each other and the odd forgotten name is forgivable. But if you're particularly rubbish, eventually you find yourself holding conversations with the odd nameless face, months down the line, by which time it's just too late to ask them outright, and then one of your other friends demands an introduction and then you've got a wee bit of a situation on your hands.

A great technique for remembering names is to create some sort of contrived link between the person's name and a feature of their face, body or personality. For instance, Rose has a giant nose; Peter is fat – he's clearly a Happy Eater. Admittedly, the technique is a tad offensive, so try to keep your personal adaptations to yourself.

special friends

In freshers' week, you will inevitably bond with a person that turns out to be a case study for your personal portfolio of poor judgements of character: you meet someone who lives on your corridor, you form an instant and unfathomable bond, you share your life aspirations and plan to tour the world together someday. But sooner or later you figure out that your friendship was built on desperation and, now you've had time to meet your real friends, you drift apart. Unfortunately, living in the same building means you are unlikely to escape this person fully. Should your relationship have ended on grim terms, this can be quite uncomfortable until enough time passes for the new, distanced acquaintanceship to become comfortable and past indiscretions to be forgotten. There are a variety of techniques that you can adopt to avoid talking to this person whenever you pass them in the corridor or around campus: pretend you're on your mobile, make out like you're late for a seminar, or – if all else fails – crack a grin, say hello and keep on walking. Slowing down will only instigate conversation.

There is a tendency amongst those in halls of residence to partake in the odd bit of bedroom shenanigans with a neighbour. This is commonly known as 'shagging on your doorstep' and is universally acclaimed to be a bad idea. But if we all abstained from acting on bad ideas then *Big Brother* would have been axed after the first series. If you're lucky, a bit of extracurricular activity down the corridor might be the start of a beautiful relationship developing into marriage and children, old age, Alzheimer's and colostomy bags, but if your drunken fumble didn't land you in the arms of a potential soul mate, then you may have got yourself in an embarrassing situation that will present itself in the corridor day after day. The techniques listed above also work in this situation, but the best thing to do is smile and breeze on by with all the confidence of an old pro. Looking nervous or embarrassed is the only thing that will make this situation uncomfortable for either of you. If, on the other hand, the odd bit of bedroom shenanigans with a neighbour becomes a whistle-stop tour of the entire corridor, then you really are an old pro. You must be very proud.

networking

An easier life in halls comes to those who take a little time to network within the establishment – developing a good rapport with certain staff members can only work in your favour. Achieving a mutually positive relationship with some staff members may, however, prove to be difficult. Generally, those who are employed by the university accommodations office, particularly those in administration or student welfare, tend to develop an intense aversion to students, so it can be difficult to get on their good side. It is best, therefore, to focus your efforts on maintenance and security staff – this is where the real perks come from and they're far easier to win over; all it takes is a touch of charm and the odd chocolate Hobnob.

the security guard / porter

At some point, you will lock yourself out of your room. Your halls security guard probably has to deal with dozens of such incidents every day, and no matter how much you simper and smirk, they'll still look at you as though you are the dumbest person in the entire universe. A grumpy porter will also be the first to clear the room as soon as a party gets a little bit rowdy (otherwise known as 'the bit where the party starts to get good'). But the security guard is there for your safety, so it's a good idea to be nice to them and make them feel appreciated. Be subtle; smile and say hello, occasionally ask 'How are you today?' and, most importantly, occasionally offer them a doughnut from the box you just bought when you oh-so-coincidentally just happened to be passing by the porter's lodge and thought you'd stop to collect your mail. Once you're on conversational terms with your security guard, you'll find you get a quicker response in locked-out situations and your parties could be nark free.

the cleaner

The cleaner in halls of residence is a complex being with immense power and an alarming degree of access. When the cleaner knocks at your bedroom door, there is very little time to respond before you hear that deathly clicking sound of the skeleton key penetrating the latch. If you don't act fast, the cleaner can and will waltz in to your room when you're in any state of undress or in any compromising position. A swift but simple 'Sorry, it's not really convenient right now' shouted through the door before they've had a chance to put the key in usually does the trick. Or if you're particularly well organised, a note on the door may suffice.

The presence of a cleaner in halls of residence works mainly to force students into keeping their rooms relatively tidy rather than to physically provide a cleaning service – the cleaner will appear on a regular basis, and for fear of being reprimanded, the student will tidy their room in preparation. To become immune to this bullying tactic, it is a good idea to work on your relationship with the cleaner. Smile, make them feel welcome, and share an occasional conversation. Offer them a cookie. Thoughtful gestures demonstrate that you appreciate all their hard work, and then they'll let you off the hook when the state of your bedroom is less than acceptable. Which, of course, would never happen…

your room

In halls of residence, your bedroom should serve as your own private sanctum in an otherwise overtly social environment, but a small number of unfortunates end up getting plonked in a shared room. It's not an ideal situation, but sometimes living in a shared room can be fun – you might end up forming a bond with someone unlike any other friendship you've ever had. Alternatively, you might end up living with the lovechild of Jar Jar Binks and Janet Street-Porter.

The key to living with a less than likeable roommate is learning how to coexist. People have different standards and priorities depending on their upbringing and personality, and behaviour that your roommate finds acceptable might be your idea of a nightmare (and vice versa). Try to be flexible and understanding. If your music tastes differ, use headphones. If your levels of cleanliness and personal hygiene differ, define clearly exclusive parts of the room and invest in some air freshener. Keep conjugal visits to your partner's abode, or explain to your roommate that you need the room to yourself and if they refuse to leave, sit on their head until they change their mind. Most importantly, make friends who are willing to let you stay over at their place when you get drunk, if you're worried that staggering into the room at 3 a.m. and waking your roomie for the fifth time this week will provoke them finally to brandish the large kitchen knife that you're pretty sure they've got hidden under their pillow.

Alternatively, if it's you who's getting annoyed at your roommate's unsociable behaviour, take a moment to explain to them calmly and honestly what's upsetting you, rather than just getting stressed and whinging about it to your friends. If nothing changes, you could always apply to move to a new room. But think very carefully about what could be done to remedy the situation, because your new roommate might be even worse.

Now that we're all respectful and harmonious with our nearest and dearest, let's take a look at some of the other common features of the halls of residence bedroom, be it shared or exclusively yours.

the sink

The vast majority of rooms in halls of residence contain a sink. Obviously, this is a highly convenient commodity to have in one's bedroom – it's always nice to know that your toothbrush is safe. The temptation, however, to use the sink as a vessel for drunken vomiting often leads to severe blockage, and it is widely renowned that there is no elegant way of dealing with sink 'vomage'. So, if you feel the chunks start to rise, try to make it to the toilet. But if you know you just won't make it, at least you've got your trusty Marigolds.

Sinks can also begin to look suspiciously like urinals when viewed through goggles of the beer variety. The less said about that, the better.

the noise

Another common design feature of university accommodation is the paper-thin walls. Eventually, you become used to a regular level of noise coming from all directions, but if you're a particularly light sleeper you might want to invest in some earplugs. These may not be 100 per cent effective, however, against a heavy onslaught of full-volume thrash metal coming from a neighbouring room during the wee small hours.

Bear in mind that there are good and bad ways of dealing with the perpetrator. Banging on the walls, ceiling or floor is a particularly bad idea; it's offensive, disrespectful and it will only start a war. The best thing to do is go over to the source of the noise, knock on the door and politely ask them to turn the volume down. The key is to be polite but firm – if you're too meek and simpering they'll just ignore you, but if you're overly aggressive they'll be more inclined to want to piss you off some more.

However, in the case of unsociably loud sex noises (with or without the accompaniment of loud music), you may not feel it is appropriate to knock on the door. Wait until the next day and just tell them outright that they were being too loud – they'll be so embarrassed you probably won't hear a peep out of them for weeks. If you're too nervous to go and talk to them face to face, write them a little note and post it under the door.

the fire alarm

The first time you are woken by the fire alarm at three in the morning is a special experience. The noise is so loud, so abrupt and so unfamiliar that it rips you out of your peaceful slumber and you catapult out of bed in a style reminiscent of the departure of a Ridley Scott alien from an unsuspecting abdomen. Then you stagger, bleary-eyed, amongst a procession of bewildered students into the rainy night, where you stand for what seems like an eternity while the fire crew arrives, marvels at the distinct lack of smoke, berates the idiot who was burning crumpets and then leaves, cursing you all for wasting their time.

A few months down the line, the familiar sound of the fire alarm merely echoes in the distance of your favourite dreamtime adventure. Ultimately, though, you still end up in the rain. So, it's a good idea to keep a dressing gown or a coat to hand for such instances, and a pair of shoes or flip-flops.

Once you get over the initial shock, late night fire alarms can be fun. For instance, the impromptu mass room exodus is a great opportunity to find out who is secretly sleeping with whom. If you're the one with the secret rendezvous, the game isn't so much fun. But at least you're getting some!

the dead plant

Every proper student bedroom contains a pathetic-looking, brown-leaved houseplant. Some view it as an essential memento mori, others merely see it as a lack of commitment to plant care on the part of the student. If you don't want your little green friend to become symbolic of life's futility, be sure to read the care instructions carefully and follow them to the letter. The main killer of houseplants is faulty growing conditions; a plant that enjoys shady conditions will suffer on the windowsill, so do your research and situate the little blighter accordingly. A bonsai tree purchased from a market stall, however, will probably die regardless of where you keep it; bonsai require a high level of care and the cheap ones are often in poor condition on the day of purchase, even though they might appear to be healthy.

the common room

Ah, the common room. The unrivalled gathering place. The room in which you and your student chums bask in each other's love and wallow in each other's filth. A fair amount of dirty crockery can and will accumulate in the common room, but it's usually nothing that can't be transferred straight into the kitchen. And it's important to remember that a situation is never too grim as long as you've got your trusty rubber gloves.

tough decision: *weakest link* or *neighbours*

Trying to appease everybody during television time can be tricky. Watching your personal choice of programming on your own TV, or commandeering the one in your neighbour's room, are effective but somewhat antisocial methods. Taking a vote is always an option, but there's no reason why deciding what to watch can't be entertaining in itself. Suggest various competitive sports to aid the decision: cockfighting, mud wrestling, pig racing, a race around the world in hot-air balloons – the possibilities are endless. Of course, these methods are fairly time-consuming and may result in you missing the disputed slot altogether, so if all else fails: rock, paper, scissors.

parties

Parties in halls are the best kind. When you hold a party in your own house, you spend the entire evening worrying about whether or not there'll be any lasting damage and how it will affect your precious deposit, but in halls the conditions are usually quite scummy anyway, so a party makes little real impact. Plus, you're guaranteed a decent turn out because you've got the population of the entire building to invite! But if you do host a party, it is your responsibility to clean up afterwards, so be ready with lots of bin liners and stain remover.

the bathroom

Ah, the delights of sharing a bathroom with a bunch of minging strangers. Essentially, the bathroom should never become particularly filthy because of the efforts of the lovely cleaner, but don't expect it to ever be overly clean, either. Students have the ability to shed some seriously random and disgusting things in the bath or shower, and in the 24–48 hours between visits from the cleaner, all sorts of peculiar little delights can attach themselves to the various enamelled surfaces. To ensure that you can use the bathroom facilities without performing the 'ick dance' (that's hopping from side to side yelling 'oh my god, oh my god, what is that on my toe?!!!') remember to bring your flip-flops and washbag, as listed in Chapter One's packing guide.

Knowing that your bare feet aren't touching the floor or the surface of the bath is blissfully comforting, so a cheap pair of flip-flops to wear in the shower is essential. You've probably already sussed that it's really not a good idea to leave any of your toiletries in the bathroom, so a little bag in which to keep them makes the journey between your room and the bathroom a little more straightforward. If you're walking from the shower to your bedroom, trying to maintain your dignity with a towel whilst simultaneously struggling to keep hold of your slippery bottles of shampoo, conditioner and body wash along with all the countless other 'essentials' that accompany your visits to the bathroom, well, you might end up revealing a little too much of yourself to your neighbours.

rinse it down

If your shower head is fixed to the wall (so you can't use it to rinse down the surfaces), you might want to keep some sort of liquid holding vessel to hand, like a beaker or a jug. Because one day, you'll go into the bathroom, and there will be little curly hairs all over the shower. And regardless of the fact you've got your faithful flip-flops, the remnants of someone's groin deforestation session is a little much for you to bear. So just fill your vessel with water from the taps and sploosh it all away!

hair in the plughole

A more regular hairy little treat often waits in the plughole. The best thing to do is take some toilet paper and use it to scoop up the hair and goop, then just stick it in the bin or the loo. Occasionally, some delightfully thoughtful person will remove the clump of hair from the drain and leave it in the corner of the bath or shower. If you've got bad eyesight you might be mistaken into thinking it's either a giant spider or a very small turd. Of course, it might actually be a giant spider or a very small turd, so it's best to just dispose of it swiftly with some toilet paper and not give it too much thought.

stage fright

Getting used to using a toilet in a strange environment can be difficult, especially if it's the first time you've lived away from home. You're sat there on the loo, and you're absolutely dying to eject last night's dinner, but you can hear people talking in the corridor and you're absolutely convinced that if they hear a splash then the world will actually just end. A simple, but somewhat ecologically unsound solution, is to take a length of toilet roll, scrunch it up, drop it in the bowl and hey presto – you've got your very own splash muffler. And for smell limitation, crack open a window and deploy a double flush.

Giant toilet blockages aren't uncommon in halls of residence, and in a perfect world the culprit would deal with the situation themselves, but sometimes you just have to take matters into your own hands... not literally, because that would be disgusting. A wire coat-hanger is the perfect tool – and a strong constitution is essential.

In summary, life in halls is colourful and full of interesting smells. When it's over, you'll miss it, so keep a cool head, learn to deal with the dirt in your own special way, and just enjoy yourself!

chapter seven:

from halls of residence to house of pestilence

many students living in halls for their first year move into private accommodation for the subsequent years of their degree. Why? Is it perhaps that living in halls is so foul an experience that students cannot stand it for any longer than a year? Hardly – life in halls is remarkably easy and stress free compared with other types of accommodation. The fact is that the majority of universities guarantee places in halls of residence to their first year students, so after that, you're kicked out onto the street to make way for the fresh young faces of the future. A lucky few will manage to cling to the teat of university accommodation for as long as possible, but the vast majority of you will, at this juncture, enter into the delightful world of the student house / flat share.

f·r·i·e·n·d·s

The typical house / flat share scenario begins with a group of students becoming bestest-best friends and deciding to shack up together when their time in halls is over. These people might be from your course, they might be some random hippies you met in the SU bar, or they might well be the people with whom you have lived for an entire year in halls of residence. But however familiar you are with each other, don't assume that you know what it will be like to share a house with these people. You never really know a person until you have lived with them in a real-life house with a landlord and leccy bills and mould and creepy crawlies. With that in mind, it can be rather difficult to predict accurately who will be a good housemate and who will turn out to be a perfect candidate for one of those reality shows where they go into someone's house and show them how to wipe their own arse while their nearest and dearest cry tears of joy.

Ask yourself a few questions about the individuals with whom you wish to live: have any of these people ever asked to borrow money from you and then failed to pay it back? Have any of these people managed to sneak off with 60 per cent or more of your entire DVD collection and never return it? Do any of these people generally emit an unpleasant odour? Have you agreed to live with one particular person who, for some unknown reason, nobody else wants to live with? If you have answered yes to any of these questions, a tiny alarm bell should be ringing. But that alarm bell is usually muffled by the great squidgy cushion of friendship, so against your better judgement you end up living with an eejit. Not to worry – whatever happens, you'll always be protected by...

the contingency plan

Once you've agreed to get a house together, it's vital that you and your friends sit down and discuss exactly what will happen if one of you pulls out of the tenancy agreement. Your contract will be on either a single or a joint basis, and, in the latter case, if one person fails to pay the rent, it is the responsibility of everyone else in the house to find the money. If one of you quits his or her degree and goes back home to Mummy and Daddy, who will be made responsible for finding a replacement housemate; the person leaving or those remaining? Who would pay the rent in the period between that person leaving and the arrival of the new housemate? You also need to discuss what you will do if someone simply can't afford to pay the rent or the bills. The landlord might ask each of you to provide a guarantor, which is a person who will be liable to pay your rent should you fail to do so. Who will be your guarantor?

a note to the lone ranger

For whatever reason, you've got nobody to live with and you can't get into university accommodation. But never fear, there are always loads of students in private houses looking for a new housemate to fill the void left by 'the one that went AWOL', and these people are very rarely psychopaths. But if you are all by your lonesome and looking for private accommodation, it is a good idea to take a buddy along to house viewings or to make sure that somebody knows exactly where you are going, just to be safe. In addition to the methods of finding accommodation listed below, you can always put up some posters advertising the fact that you are looking for a house. You never know, a house might just find you!

finding a house

Try to get some advice from older students – who are the reputable landlords and letting agents in your area and who are the dodgy, no good scoundrels? Where are the best locations? However, don't make too many decisions about your 'ideal house' in the initial stages, because being too selective might cause you to overlook a really good property. It's best to keep an open mind – that way you avoid disappointment when you can't find the house that perfectly matches your exact criteria. The most important things to bear in mind when you start searching are the number of bedrooms you need, the maximum weekly rent you can afford, and your favoured location.

take a walk

Start your search by taking a walk or a bus ride through some of the areas that are big on student housing. While you're exploring, look out for 'To Let' signs and make a note of the name of the letting agent and their contact details. Above all, observe the location – are there many local shops or pubs? How far are you from the university? What are the local bus routes? If you were to get sick of your housemates, how far would you have to travel in order to escape? Is there an abundance of graffiti on all the buildings? Once you've got a feel for the locations, you will have a better idea of which houses might be more suitable when you search through the various listings.

the university accommodation service

Many university accommodation services provide a private housing search facility – it might be a bulletin or message board or an online database of housing. This is a good place to start, because the university will probably only advertise for registered, reputable landlords. Probably.

Internet accommodation services

There are a good few online services to help you find somewhere to live, and you can find them easily by simply typing 'student housing' into a search engine. But be aware that some sites are less well known to the landlords and therefore far less comprehensive. Take a look at Appendix B for a recommended site.

local accommodation agencies and estate agents

These agencies will charge you a fee for their services, so bear this in mind and be sure to ask about extra charges. They can only charge you after you have decided to sign a contract on one of their houses, so never pay any money upfront. And remember – estate agents tend to be pathological liars, so take everything they say with a pinch of salt.

local newspapers

Private landlords often advertise in local newspapers, but they aren't necessarily regulated by the same guidelines as the university accommodation service or an estate agent, so be extra vigilant and try to view the property as a group.

When you find a place you like the sound of, act quickly to arrange a viewing. But don't put all your eggs in one basket – keep an open mind and arrange several viewings of different properties. When you view a house, consider the following questions:

- Are all the rooms furnished?

- How does the house smell? Any signs of damp or mould?

- Are there valid gas safety certificates for all gas appliances?

- Is there a smoke detector, carbon monoxide detector, fire extinguisher and / or fire blanket?

- What appliances are included in the rent? Is there a fridge, freezer, oven, washing machine? (Also check that these are in working order; if not, inquire as to when the landlord will have them fixed.)

- How is the house heated – central heating, electric fan heaters, gas heaters?

- What are the rooms like? Is the smallest, dingiest bedroom suitable for human habitation? (Some poor sucker will have to draw the short straw.)

- How old are the mattresses on the beds? If they are old and bumpy, is there any chance they could be replaced?

- Are the current tenants available for a chat? (If the landlord or letting agent seems to have a problem with you talking to the residents, that's probably a bad sign.)

- Is there parking space / safe bicycle storage?

- Are all the windows lockable? Are the doors secured?

- Is there anywhere to dry clothes – tumble dryer, drying rack, clothes line?

- Is the house smoking or non-smoking? (If your group is a mixture of smokers and non-smokers, you might want to discuss this issue amongst yourselves.)

- Is there a garden? Are you responsible for its upkeep?

- Is the house situated next to a public footpath that is littered with used condoms and hypodermic needles?

- Are there any dead bodies buried under the patio?

Once you've given the place a look and you've started to fall for its grubby charms, you need to find out the following from the landlord or letting agent:

- What is the length of the let (i.e. how long will you be allowed to live in the house)? If it's a full year, will there be a discount for the holiday period? (Some landlords do this, but it is fairly rare.)
- Double check the rent. How much is it per week? How is it payable? Per week, per month, per term?

- Could the rent vary depending on the size of the individual's room? (This might be something you can organise with the landlord, or you could make an agreement amongst yourselves – just make sure it's fair!)

- How much is the deposit? When will you get it back? (You'll have to pay a deposit when you sign the contract, and you won't get it back until you've moved out of the house.)

- Are any bills included in the rent (i.e. gas, water, electricity)?

- What bills will you have to pay yourselves and how much is this likely to add to the weekly rent?

- Will you need to provide a guarantor?

- Will the landlord supply an inventory of all the items within the house for you to check over?

- Which companies currently supply the gas, electricity and water? Will these all still be connected when you move in?

- Is there a telephone line?

Once you've decided that you really like a place and you're all committed, it's time to show the landlord or letting agent that you're not total idiots. A dodgy landlord will happily try to take advantage of your youth and naivety and rip you off good and proper, so you always need to be one step ahead, particularly if you ever want to see your deposit again. Always be polite in your dealings with the landlord or letting agent, but in the back of your mind, assume that everything they say is lies and that they are, in fact, the living spawn of Satan.

the contract and your rights

There are lots of different types of tenancy agreement, but the most common for a bunch of students renting from a private landlord (who doesn't live in the house) is an assured shorthold tenancy. The main benefit of this type of tenancy is that you have the right to control your home – the landlord can't walk in unannounced but must give you notice before a visit. It also means that your landlord is legally obliged to maintain the roof, guttering, walls, windows and doors, and the gas, electricity, heating, water and sanitation systems. However, it is fairly easy for the landlord to evict you in this type of tenancy agreement, so be good little children and keep paying the rent!

When you receive the contract, you have to be given time to read it over. Unless you are absolutely sure that you understand every single word of its terms, you must show it to someone from the university accommodation service or from the Citizens' Advice Bureau – they will be able to inform you if any of the terms are unusual or unacceptable, and advise you of what to do in such an instance.

You should also do a bit of research on your local area (the Internet is always a good place to start) to find out what rules and regulations are supposed to govern your landlord. For instance, a rule has recently been introduced with the intent to raise the standard of private housing for tenants like you (note that this doesn't cover university halls of residence!). Any landlord owning a property that is three or more storeys high and is occupied by five or more non-related tenants needs an HMO (houses of multiple occupancy) license. Some local housing authorities are also allowed to demand that landlords of smaller HMOs possess a license if the area is known for particularly poor standards of housing, so it's worth doing your research to find out what the regulations are in your area and whether or not the house you wish to move into, or already live in, is affected. Your local housing authority should have a register available where you can find out whether or not your particular property is licensed. If you find that your landlord should have a license, but doesn't, they are breaking the law and, if they are caught, they could be charged anything up to £20,000. Just remember, in the world of the landlord–tenant relationship, knowledge is power!

Anyway, back to the contract. When you've agreed to its terms, each of you will sign the contract, and you should be given a copy to keep. It's a good idea to elect a responsible person (or at least someone who knows the difference between a filing cabinet and a wheelie bin) to keep together all your house documentation. Also, remember that as a student, you are not eligible to pay council tax, but you might each have to provide a certificate proving your exemption – you can get one of these from university administration. Once you get them, get the responsible person to keep them all together with the paperwork.

moving in!

It's a good idea to divvy up the rooms before you actually move into the house, unless you want moving day to turn into a frenzied land-rush. Here's a suggested method that has worked (sort of) in the past: each take a piece of paper and write down your first, second and third choice of room. Anyone whose first choice is uncontested gets the room. Two people who have the same first choice can battle it out over a fearsome game of Twister or a Marmite eating contest, and the loser has to accept their second choice. If their second choice is already taken because it was somebody else's first choice, then they must move on to their third choice, and so on. It's a complicated system and it's full of flaws, but at least this way some people get the room they really wanted, and those who get the rubbish rooms only have themselves to blame.

When you move into the house, you need to get the landlord to show you the location of the following things:

• the gas meter

• the electricity meter

• the water meter

• the fuse box

• the water stopcock (for turning off the water supply)

• the gas tap (for turning off the gas supply)

• the thermostat

• the central heating controls

• the water heating controls

You'll need to take readings from the gas meter, the electricity meter and the water meter, so you know exactly where you stand if a bill arrives for energy used by the previous tenants. You also need to call the current suppliers (or contact new suppliers should you wish to change companies) and give them a contact name for billing (see the paragraph about bills below) and tell them the meter reading. At some point you should also call the local council and find out what day the bins are emptied and where you need to leave yours for collection.

the inventory

Your landlord should provide an inventory, listing all the items in the house and their current condition. Check every single item on the list. If anything is missing, make a note on the inventory and then inform the landlord immediately. Then, go around the house and take photographs of every room, marking the state of the house when you entered it (if you can get your hands on a digital camera this is ideal as you won't have to pay for any processing). Then, at the end of your tenancy, you can use the photos as a reference to return the house to its original state, and then your landlord will have no reason to keep back any of your deposit!

life in the house

Having been so learned and wise in your search for a house, you've put yourself in the best possible position for a stress-free existence. But sadly, no amount of planning is ever going to stop you and your housemates from getting on each other's nerves. You can, however, take measures to ensure (to some extent, at least) that the bills get paid on time...

bills

In the most extreme circumstance (i.e. none of the bills are included in the rent), you'll have to pay the gas, electricity and water bills, plus the phone bill and the television license. Each of you should take responsibility for at least one bill, and have that particular service registered in your name. That way, everyone gets their turn at being the one to bully people for money.

To minimise bills (and to be kinder to the environment) try to get into the habit of being ecological: invest in energy saving light bulbs, don't fill the kettle to the top if you're only making one cup of tea, turn off the lights when you're not in a room, and switch the electrical appliances off at the unit or the wall rather than leaving them on standby. Only use the washing machine when you've got enough dirty clothes for a full load, take showers instead of baths, and turn off the tap when you are brushing your teeth. Keep the thermostat to a reasonable setting, and, if you feel cold, think about how sensible it is to wear shorts and a T-shirt in the middle of winter before turning up the heating. All these little things add up to make a significant difference to your bills, and then you'll have more money for partying.

The most complicated bill is, undoubtedly, the phone bill. It is highly unlikely that you and your housemates will be happy to split its total equally, since some will have used the phone more than others. Should you be the one in charge of the phone bill, you will probably try to get your housemates to keep a record of their calls by positioning some sort of log sheet or book, complete with pencil-on-a-string, in the vicinity of the telephone. But lo and behold, the day the itemised bill arrives, you discover that a little phone pixie has mischievously been making dozens of random calls to numbers that don't appear to have been logged! All parties deny any knowledge of the mystery phone calls, and another little chip of your equanimity flies off into the ether to join the other fragments of your once placid demeanour. The solution? Don't be the one in charge of the phone bill.

security

Treat the contents of your student house like you would treat the contents of your car: do not leave expensive items on display in front of the windows. Student houses are a target for theft because they're always full of laptops and iPods, and if left on display they're just easy pickings. So don't do it. Also, be sure to lock windows and doors when you are out of the house, or at night when you are all sleeping. And make sure you have room insurance!

house party! yeah!

If you decide to have a party in your house, it's a good idea to visit the neighbours beforehand and let them know, just in case they take offence to the unexpected noise and you end up getting an ASBO or something. If you're feeling particularly friendly you could even invite them.

To prepare for a party, remove anything remotely fragile or valuable from any of the party rooms and stick them all together in a room that won't be used, like a top floor bedroom or even an airing cupboard. In preparation for the big clean-up that inevitably follows any good party, make sure you've got a good supply of stain remover, fabric deodoriser, bin liners and, of course, your faithful rubber gloves. If there is a huge catastrophe during the party, such as someone flattening your dining table or falling through a dividing wall, just drink lots of alcohol and then worry about it in the morning.

bug attack

The best way of avoiding an infestation of insects or vermin is simply to keep the house clean. As shocking as this may sound, if there are no scraps of food lying about, they will not come. But, should all attempts to familiarise your token slobby housemate with the finer points of 'cleaning up after oneself' fail dismally, and your house does eventually become infested with insects, stop screaming, buy some insect repellent or a humane mouse trap, then call the landlord and get them to call in the pest control people. Don't attempt to handle the problem by yourself and don't think that there will be any humane ways of getting rid of bugs (I once heard of an attempt to lure ants out of an infested kitchen by laying down a trail of sugar that led out of the door. Not surprisingly, this merely attracted more ants to the scene). If you are worried about hurting the little creatures, bear in mind that they're all calling you names behind your back, and one of them did a poo on your omelette. Finally, do not give your resident vermin names, as you will only become upset when pest control arrives and little Algernon meets an untimely end.

the house meeting

You know it's all gone wrong when someone knocks on the wall mid-argument and says, 'OK, come on guys, house meeting.' The term 'house meeting' just carries negative connotations, but sometimes it's vital that you all sit down and have a frank and open discussion about who owes money to whom, who hasn't done any washing-up since the shock spoon-in-suds incident three months ago, and whose boyfriend is living in the house rent free and grossing everyone out by walking around with no clothes on. While it might be difficult to organise around your various rock and roll lifestyles, the occasional house meeting is essential. Should you wish to organise a house meeting, try advertising its time and location with a poster campaign across the house. Remember: if you bug them, they will come.

the kitchen

It's about time we returned to the scene of the grime (oh dear). Now, as you're probably aware, the house kitchen is, in some respects, quite a different affair to that in halls of residence. While the halls kitchen is shared by a large number of students whose dysfunctional relationship is forged from their forced cohabitation, the house kitchen is shared by an intimate group of friends whose dysfunctional relationship stems from their conscious decision to live with one another. Plus the house kitchen suffers from a detrimental lack of professional cleaning staff. The mess and dirt in a house kitchen, therefore, can not only become worse than that in a halls kitchen but, in the increased intimacy of the circumstances, it can lead to more personal modes of blame shifting and character assassination.

On a more positive note, however, in the environment of a house it is far easier to economise on your food budget and on space in the fridge and cupboards by buying essential items, such as milk and bread, communally. There are many systems you can adopt to make sure that everyone contributes equally, but bear in mind that different methods work for different households. Some houses, for instance, choose to each make a contribution towards a house kitty, which is then used to buy the essentials as and when is necessary. This does, however, require the force of one individual to collect money from people when the kitty is empty, and it also requires a certain degree of trust – you need to know that nobody will bugger off with the kitty money and spend it all on sweets.

THE SHOPPING SHEET					
	MILK (PER LITRE)	BREAD	BUTTER	CLEANING PRODUCTS	BOG ROLL
DEREK	卌 I	卌 II	II	IIII	III
SIMON	卌 卌 II	卌 I	III	I	IIII
TRISH	卌 II	卌 III	II	II	IIII
GENEVIEVE	III	III	I	卌 IIII	卌 卌 卌 III

There is also the 'take it in turns' system, where each of you takes it in turns (the clue was in the name, really) to buy the communal items. But this system also requires some degree of organisation, and it's more than likely to end up with a weekly repeat of someone standing by the empty bread bin screaming, 'Whose turn is it to buy the bread?' In a house where you all have different timetables, different lifestyles and different organisational skills, the best system is a flexible system, like the Shopping Sheet.

So it's very simple – you draw one of these in pretty coloured felt tips, stick it on the kitchen wall along with the obligatory pencil-on-a-string, and then every time anyone makes a purchase they add a notch to their tally. The sheet provides a tangible record of who has purchased what, so you can see who is lagging behind and then bully them into coughing up some cash. But the system is also very flexible – in the pictured chart, it seems that Genevieve hardly ever buys any milk. But what she has neglected in milk, she has made up for in cleaning products and toilet paper.

The Shopping Sheet is easily adaptable to your own personal situation. For instance, you might all drink a lot of tea, so you should have tea on your list. Whatever you choose to buy communally, the sheet means that you have the freedom to buy each item as and when it is needed, and if one person isn't contributing their fair share, the evidence is there for everyone to see and that person can be rolled up in a carpet and boiled in a vat of yak's wee.

cleaning the house

It's not until you live in a shared house that you realise how much you underappreciated the work of your halls cleaner. Mess and dirt just piles up and, unless you are all naturally tidy people and stay on top of the issue, you might find that your entire house begins to resemble some sort of Tracey Emin installation (with a touch more class, obviously). Some people believe that drawing up a rota will keep the house tidy, but a rota only works when accompanied by the guiding influence of an enforcer; a person who is imperious enough to ensure that everyone does their allotted work. So, if you're all too apathetic to take on the role of Britain's next top despot, there is a less regimented solution: the Chores Chart. And yes, alliteration is an essential part of domestic motivation.

The system works on the exact same basis as the Shopping Sheet and, again, you can adjust the categories to suit your own personal needs. Note that washing your own dishes should never be included, because that's something people should bloody well do without need for applause or universal recognition.

the bathroom

First of all, let it be said that when you share a house with friends, you inevitably end up talking about your bowel movements. But this increased intimacy means that the toilet-based faux pas generally fails to go unnoticed. For instance, in a house toilet, a giant floater is no longer the anonymous nuisance that it was in halls; in the smaller environment, the identity of the culprit is always revealed in the end. Remember that there is no longer a cleaner, so failure to act on a toilet-tastrophe can become very unpleasant. Also remember that the toilet brush is there to be used – it is not a decorative ornament. But having said that, never, ever use the toilet brush in a full bowl; always flush the toilet first, use the brush, then flush the toilet again to clean the brush. Spread the word on this one, because dirty toilet brushes are NOT PLEASANT.

THE CHORES CHART						
	WASHING OTHER PEOPLE'S DISHES	CLEANING THE KITCHEN	CLEANING THE BATHROOM	CLEANING THE LIVING ROOM	VACUUMING HALLWAYS + STAIRS	EMPTYING THE BIN
DEREK	ｌﾞﾟ ｌﾞﾟ			١		ｌﾞﾟ ｌﾞﾟ
SIMON	ⅠⅠⅠ		١			١
TRISH	ｌﾞﾟ ⅠⅠⅠⅠ	١				
GENEVIEVE	ⅠⅠ					

love thy landlord

Any time something in the house breaks or malfunctions, you should call the landlord immediately and inform them of the problem. Sometimes, however, landlords can be a little slow when it comes to rushing to your aid, particularly if it isn't anything as urgent as a burst water main or a gas leak. Landlords don't tend to move very quickly unless there's a profit to be made or a huge loss of money on the horizon, so if, for instance, your washing machine has broken, you might have to become quite persistent with your phone calls before it gets fixed.

Should you encounter any ongoing problems with the house or the landlord, it is best to make a record of all your communication; note the date and time of all your phone conversations and make photocopies of all written correspondence. It sounds slightly over the top, but should you end up with a horrible landlord, any material evidence that can prove your good intentions as a tenant will stand you in good stead in the event of a dispute over the return of your deposit at the end of the tenancy.

It's not unusual for landlords to find twisted little techniques to withhold your deposit money, so do yourself a favour by protecting yourself in the following ways:

- Prevent the development of mould and rising damp by airing out the house (i.e. opening a window or two) a couple of times a week. If there were no discernible signs of damp when you moved in, the landlord can decide to hold you responsible for anything that develops during your tenancy. (Obviously, don't leave the windows open when the house is empty, because that would be silly.)

- Try to keep the house relatively clean and tidy, or at least clean it from top to bottom before your tenancy expires.
- Make sure that spillages and stains on the carpets or furniture are dealt with swiftly. Stain remover is your friend.

- Only ever use tiny blobs of Blu Tack on the walls, and try to use the white, stain-proof variety. When you need to remove it, roll a bigger ball of Blu Tack over the blob, and it should come off gently without damaging any paintwork. If it has left a stain, you can wash it away with sugar-soap (available from hardware stores). Too much sugar soap will actually remove the paint, but as long as the Blu Tack grease is gone, you can touch up the spot on the wall using a tester pot of paint. Do bear in mind that this whole business is very risky, and if want to avoid a lot of fuss, just don't use Blu Tack on the walls. Ask your landlord if you can use drawing pins, or put up some picture hooks instead.

- Clean the oven occasionally. (In my first, rather scummy house, we never cleaned the oven and I'm pretty sure the people who lived there before us never cleaned it either. One day the oven caught on fire, purely due to the fact that it was so gross inside, and we all had to pay for a new one from our deposits. It was very upsetting. So, clean the oven.)

- If you do happen to damage anything in the house and it cannot be fixed, tell the landlord immediately and get them to quote the amount that will be deducted from your deposit. That way, you know exactly where you stand and the landlord can't take advantage of the situation once you have left the house.

If, at the end of your tenancy, your landlord is too busy rolling around the floor of their mansion, clutching their beloved moneybags and laughing maniacally, to pay back your deposit, you should write to them and ask for a detailed breakdown of the amount withheld and the alleged reason. If you don't agree with their response, go to your local Citizens' Advice Bureau. If they think you've been done over, they can provide you with the appropriate forms you need to take the blighter to the small claims court. If, however, you ritualistically burnt the coffee table and used its ashes to mark out the shape of a giant phallus on the living room floor, you might just have to live without the deposit.

And on that happy note, we come to the end of this whirlwind tour of *chez* student. So, as you embark upon your undergraduate adventure, remember that the university experience is not just educational, but also essential for personal growth and development. At best you will leave university as a mature, well-balanced individual with a fine qualification and a close circle of friends, and at worst you will come out of the whole experience riddled with deep-seated psychological disorders. Either way, it's all character building. Enjoy!

appendix a:

the substitution guide

No method of food preparation is beyond your reach, despite how minimal your kitchen supplies may be. If you're trying to follow a recipe but you're missing a vital instrument, consult this list to see if there is an alternative within your grasp.

BAKING TRAY	Use a roasting tin, an ovenproof dish or a cleverly moulded sheet of tin foil.
BISCUIT CUTTERS	Use a glass or a cup as a guide and cut around it with a knife. Or make fun shapes with a bit of free-styling.
CAKE TIN	Use a baking tray and some cupcake holders to make fairy cakes instead.
CASSEROLE DISH	Use any ovenproof dish and make a lid out of tinfoil.

CHOPPING BOARD	Use a pair of scissors over a dish, or use the 'Chopping without a chopping board' technique (see Chapter Four).
COLANDER	Use a sieve. Or place a lid on the pan, tip it over the sink and then move the lid slightly to create a small gap to let the water run out. Or fish the food out of the water with a spoon or fork.
FRYING PAN	Use a saucepan or a wok.
GARLIC CRUSHER	Chop the garlic finely with a knife, or crush small pieces on a chopping board with the back of a spoon.
GRATER	Use a knife and make itty bitty little slices, then go crazy with some scissors.
GRIDDLE PAN	Use a frying pan.
LADLE	Use a spoon, or a cup, or just pour.
LEMON JUICER	Squish the lemon half using a fork. Let the juice run through a sieve to catch pulp and pips.

METAL SKEWERS	Buy some disposable wooden ones (they're very cheap). Remember to soak them in cold water for about twenty minutes before you use them, otherwise they burn.
MIXING BOWL	Use a saucepan, or just any bowl you can get your hands on. Or a jug.
MUFFIN TRAY	If you're making cupcakes or muffins, just use freestanding cupcake cases on a baking tray. If you're making Yorkshire puddings, you're a bit screwed without the right shaped tray, so just buy the frozen ready-made ones, stick them on a baking tray and hope for the best.
NUTCRACKER	Use a hammer, or a shoe, or a gun.
OVEN GLOVES	Use a FOLDED tea towel.
PASTRY BRUSH	Use your fingers (clean them first).
PEELER	Use a small sharp knife, or wash the veg under cold running water and don't bother peeling it.

PESTLE AND MORTAR	Stick the things you want to grind into a sandwich bag, wrap it in a tea towel, then whack it repeatedly with a shoe.
ROASTING TIN	Use a baking tray or an ovenproof dish.
ROLLING PIN	Use a wine bottle (empty and washed).
SPATULA	You can try using a spoon, a fork or even a knife, but nothing really matches the awesome handling power of a spatula. Sorry.
SPECIALITY KNIFE	No bread knife, carving knife, cook's knife, paring knife, boning knife or utility knife? Just use a regular knife, for crying out loud.
STEAMER	Use a sieve above a saucepan of boiling water. For more info, see 'Steaming without a steamer' (Chapter Four).
TURKEY BASTER	Use a spoon.

TONGS	Take a spoon in each hand and make a grabby-type thing, or simply use a spatula or a fork.
WHISK	Use a fork. Or you could try fashioning a whisk out of coat hangers. Probably won't work, though.
WOK	Use a frying pan or a saucepan.
WOODEN SPOON	Use a regular spoon, or a disinfected twig.

measuring equipment

Most of the time, it's easy enough to guess the quantity of an ingredient. But sometimes precise measurements are required, and this is why you need a measuring jug. If you don't have one, you should get one.

If you don't have a set of scales but you need one to measure something in grams, like sugar or flour, then as long as you have a measuring jug, all is not lost. Grams of sugar can be converted directly to millilitres – so 100 g sugar is the same as 100 ml sugar. Flour, however, is more difficult to measure in this way, because it's all airy and it doesn't sit as well as sugar. If you want accurate measurements of flour, buy a set of scales (they can be very cheap). However, if you're happy to chance it, take the required measurement in grams (e.g. 100 g) and multiply it by 1.4, thus giving you a very rough idea of the measurement in millilitres (so 100 g = approximately 140 ml). To measure, spoon your flour into the measuring jug, and tap the base on a flat surface to cause the flour to settle. This technique is by no means accurate, but do remember that you can add more flour at a later stage, but you can't take any away.

appendix b:

useful resources

handy cooking resources

The Internet is great for the curious young chef. Say, for instance, you don't know how to make scrambled eggs and you don't want to sound like a complete moron by admitting it to your friends: type in 'how to cook scrambled eggs' on a search engine, and some genius will have been kind enough to provide instructions. Be sure to include 'how to cook' in the search, otherwise you might end up on a blog about some couple in Arkansas's struggle with infertility.

www.bbc.co.uk/food/recipes
The whole BBC food website is brilliant, but on this particular page you can type in three ingredients and the database will come up with a load of recipes containing those ingredients.

www.uktvfood.co.uk
This website features thousands of recipes, all of which have appeared on the tellybox.

www.eatwell.gov.uk/healthydiet
Everything you ever wanted to know about food.

www.eatwell.gov.uk/keepingfoodsafe
Everything you ever wanted to know about how food can kill you.

www.recipes4us.co.uk/conversion_charts.htm
Sometimes, when you get recipes by doing a search on the Internet, they can use weird American measurements and cooking terms. This page has a bunch of conversion charts for all your converting needs.

general studenty stuff

National Union of Students
Anything you want or need to know about the NUS can be found on their website:

www.nusonline.co.uk

loans and finance

Residents of England and Wales Student Finance Direct
www.studentsupportdirect.co.uk
Tel: 08456 077 577

appendix b

Residents of Scotland Student Awards Agency for Scotland (SAAS)
www.saas.gov.uk
Tel: 08451 111 711

Residents of Wales Student Finance Wales
www.studentfinancewales.co.uk
Tel: 08456 028 845

Residents of Northern Ireland Student Finance NI
www.studentfinanceni.co.uk
Tel: 08456 000 662

EGAS
The Educational Grants Advisory Service is part of the Family Welfare Association. They can provide information and advice on sources of funding for students.
www.egas-online.org
Tel: 0207 2546 251

National Debtline
If it all goes a bit wrong, these people can help.
www.nationaldebtline.co.uk
Tel: 0808 808 4000

accommodation, housing and bills

Accommodationforstudents.com
This is a great online tool for searching available housing and potential housemates in your area. The site was set up by a couple of students in 2000, and for that reason it has the needs of the student at its heart and is very comprehensive. Registration is free.

www.accommodationforstudents.com

Upmystreet.com
An excellent free tool for researching your location. Type in the postcode and up pops a wealth of information about the local area, such as crime statistics, local amenities and energy price comparisons.

www.upmystreet.com

Shelter
Shelter is a non-government organisation that can provide you with help and advice regarding accommodation. This section of their website is devoted to student housing:

http://england.shelter.org.uk/advice/advice-109.cfm

They also run a free helpline:

Tel: 0808 800 4444

Citizens' Advice Bureau

A registered charity that can provide you with confidential advice about legal issues. You can find your local CAB (where you can book an appointment with a trained advisor) via their national website:

www.citizensadvice.org.uk

They also run an online advice guide:

www.adviceguide.org.uk

Energywatch

An independent gas and electricity watchdog. You can find the cheapest energy suppliers in your area on their website:

www.energywatch.org.uk

If you've had a problem with your energy supplier, and you feel like you are being treated unfairly, you can call the Energywatch helpline:

Tel: 08459 06 07 08

Ofwat

If you have problems with your water company, take a look at Ofwat's website:

www.ofwat.gov.uk

Ofcom

If you have a problem with your telecommunications supplier, check out Ofcom's website:

www.ofcom.org.uk

insurance

Endsleigh
The NUS recommends Endsleigh for room contents insurance.
www.endsleigh.co.uk
Tel: 0800 028 3571

health

NHS Direct
If your tongue's gone green and your eyeballs have fallen
out, call NHS Direct for advice:
www.nhsdirect.nhs.uk
Tel: 0845 46 47

other titles from summersdale

STUDENT GRUB

STUFFED WITH NEW RECIPES

ALASTAIR WILLIAMS

Student Grub
Alastair Williams
£5.99
ISBN 1-84024-185-3

How many takeaway pizzas and long-congealed curries will it take to convince you that, as a student, you need this book?

How much more of a hammering can your finances (not to mention your digestive system) take before you see sense?

Get real and impress your friends with the gorgeous grub that you'll produce using this book. All the basics of cooking are explained, and with popular staples, meals for one or for a (student) household, foreign foods, veggie and healthy eating sections, this book is of far more use than a lecture.

So forget about core texts: you won't regret adding this volume to your library.

De-stress for
EXAMS

summersdale *self-help*

EXAM-BUSTING TIPS

How to pass exams
the easy way

Student
DARES

Go on,
I dare you!

STEPH LITTLE

De-Stress for Exams
£2.99
ISBN 1-84024-076-8

You may have 101 textbooks about your chosen subject, but this is the only one you'll ever need on how to de-stress for your exams.

Coping with stress while taking exams can be more testing than the papers themselves. *De-stress for Exams* will ensure you enter that exam hall with a clear head and a calm attitude – essential for tackling tests with the best possible chance of success.

Exam-Busting Tips
£2.99
ISBN 1-84024-076-8

What's stopping you acing your exams? This handy little book identifies the most common stumbling blocks and is crammed with practical tips on how to overcome academic angst.

Student Dares
Steph Little
£2.99
ISBN 1-84024-451-8

Got enough traffic cones to start your own engineering company? Need some new student gags?

Class will never be the same. Play the game, if you dare...

www.studentkitchensurvival.co.uk

www.summersdale.com